Digital Processes

Planning
Design
Production

Moritz Hauschild
Rüdiger Karzel

Birkhäuser
Edition Detail

Authors:
Moritz Hauschild, Prof. Dipl.-Ing. M. Arch.
Rüdiger Karzel, Prof. Dipl.-Ing. Arch., Dipl. NDS ETHZ

Co-authors:
Martin Berchtold, Dipl.-Ing. Arch.
Klaus Bollinger, Prof. Dr.-Ing.
Manfred Grohmann, Prof. Dipl.-Ing.
Holger Heilmann, Dipl.-Ing. Arch.
Philipp Krass, Dipl.-Ing. Arch.
Arne Künstler, Dipl.-Ing.
Martin Manegold, Dipl.-Ing. Arch.
Heike Matcha, Dipl.-Ing. Arch.
Shozo Motosugi, Prof. Dr.-Ing.
Christoph Motzko, Prof. Dr.-Ing.
Oliver Tessmann, Dr.-Ing. Arch.
Axel Wirth, Prof. Dr. iur.

Staff:
Ante Ljubas
Sara Darvish
Christoph Kühne

Editor:

Editorial services:
Cornelia Hellstern, Dipl.-Ing.; Nicola Kollmann, Dipl.-Ing. Arch.; Eva Schönbrunner, Dipl.-Ing.

Editorial assistants:
Katinka Johanning, M. A.; Florian Köhler; Peter Popp, Dipl.-Ing.; Verena Schmidt, Dipl.-Ing.

Drawings:
Dejanira Bitterer, Dipl.-Ing.; Ralph Donhauser, Dipl.-Ing.;
Nicola Kollmann, Dipl.-Ing. Arch.; Elisabeth Krammer, Dipl.-Ing.

ISBN: 978-3-0346-0725-4

Printed on acid-free paper made from cellulose bleached without
the use of chlorine.

Typesetting & production:
Simone Soesters

Printed by:
Firmengruppe APPL, aprinta druck, Wemding
1st edition, 2011

This book is also available in a German language edition
(ISBN 978-3-920034-35-5).

Bibliographic information published by Die Deutsche Bibliothek.
Die Deutsche Bibliothek lists this publication in the Deutsche Nationalbibliographie;
detailed bibliographic data is available on the internet at http://dnb.ddb.de.

Institut für internationale
Architektur-Dokumentation GmbH & Co. KG
Hackerbrücke 6, 80335 Munich
Tel: +49 89 381620-0
Fax: +49 89 398670
www.detail.de

Distribution partner:
Birkhäuser GmbH
PO Box 133, 4010 Basel, Switzerland
Tel: +41.61.568 98 01
Fax: +41.61.568 98 99
e-mail: sales@birkhauser.ch
www.birkhauser.ch

DETAIL Practice
Digital Processes

Contents

7   *Introduction*
      The evolution of digital processes

      Digital planning technologies
14   Geographic information systems
16   Analysis techniques – mapping
18   Simulation and optimization
21   Computer-aided architectural design (CAAD)
24   Rule-based planning – parametrics
27   Digital capture – terrestrial laser scanning (TLS)
29   Project room – the transparent project
33   Digital interfaces in construction
41   Legal challenges in the context of digital planning processes

      Digital production technologies
46   Generative procedures
46   Rapid procedures
50   CNC precast concrete elements
50   Robot-aided assembly of individual elements
52   3D printing on a large scale
54   Subtractive procedures
56   CNC laser cutting
58   CNC jet cutting
59   CNC hot wire cutting
60   CNC milling
61   Jointed-arm robotics
62   Forming processes
64   CNC bending edges
66   CNC punching and nibbling
68   Pressure forming

      Project examples
72   Digital generation of a supporting structure
74   The Sphere at Deutsche Bank in Frankfurt
76   Pedestrian bridge in Reden
77   Rolex Learning Center in Lausanne
82   Hungerburg funicular in Innsbruck
86   National Temple of Divine Providence in Warsaw
92   Taichung Metropolitan Opera House in Taiwan

      Appendix
105   Glossary
107   Literature: reference books and articles
108   Manufacturers, companies and academic institutions
109   Picture credits
110   Index

The evolution of digital processes

1   Palazzetto dello Sport in Rome (I) 1958, Pier Luigi Nervi. The structural system was tested in a large-scale 1:10 model which was used to optimize the pre-casting of the concrete shell elements.

This book introduces the various digital processes which are employed in construction and the possibilities they offer. The reader will acquire an overview of which software-based methods can contribute to optimizing planning in which phase of a project. It is divided into three main chapters: digital planning technologies, digital production technologies and one with project examples which serve to illustrate the previously described methods. The chapter "planning technology" explains the broad spectrum of digital methods which can be deployed during the development of projects.

Costs, time frames and quality are still the challenges for all planners in every construction project. This is why the old adage states: contacts and luck plus knowledge and experience plus talent and hard work lead to success. Or in other words: "Get the job done, do it right, don't get sued." These recipes for success, which are still true today, have been added to over the years, as the transition from purely analogue ways of working to digital working methods has forced the reorganization of the design and construction process, eliminated lots of constraints, and frequently requires quick rethinking. In the course of these changes, rules and boundaries along with legal procedures also need to be clarified, as, along with the new planning technologies, come legal challenges too.

Today it is not only the architect and engineer who organize construction tasks. For this reason it is seen to be necessary to arrive at a single, seamless flow of data from the setting of objectives through the design and manufacturing to the actual implementation as part of a cohesive process. To do this the images of conventional career roles must be examined and expanded. Isolated applications become major fields of work and communal databases get fused together. Individuals will increasingly involve themselves as part of a group of specialists.

Pierre de Montreuil in the Gothic style and Filippo Brunelleschi in the Renaissance were outstanding master builders and as such were artists as well as excellent craftsmen who could make masterly use of the most important materials of the time. Industrialization brought an enormous increase in absolute knowledge with it. As early as the 19th century the conceivable technical possibilities were already so extensive, and handling them already required so much know-how, that in France they divided up this extensive new field of work, as part of the apprenticeship for the building trade, between the Écoles des Beaux-Arts and the Écoles Polytechniques: one camp concentrated on the Fine Arts, the other on the demonstrable facts. This separation meant the first deep divide in terms of professional self-identity in the construction industry. Despite this, several designers managed to assert their claim to be master builders even in the 20th century. Pointing the way ahead, amongst others, were the thoughts and buildings of Antoni Gaudí, Pier Luigi Nervi and Frei Otto, in whose cases the resulting constructions hardly allow you to conclude whether they are the work of an engineer or an architect. Their solutions work and are beautiful because of their logical and material order.

Meanwhile we talk less about the actual construction of buildings. Today's design does not focus on the completion of a product alone, but on its comprehensive life cycle. Even at the design stage, digital simulation preempts questions which come up during the construction process or the life cycle of a building.

2 Efficient dome construction with oblique reinforced concrete pillars, developed as a model, Sagrada Familia, Barcelona (E), from 1883, Antoni Gaudí
3 Lattice tower on the Oka (RUS), 1919, Vladimir Uchov. The Russian engineer experimentally developed such delicate hyper-paraboloidal rotational shells that they could only be photographed against the bright sky with difficulty.
4 Digital simulation of a suspended model with Kangaroo Physics. The program was developed by Daniel Piker and is a software add-on for the program Rhinoceros.
5 Due to the digital processes in planning and production more and more powerful solutions are becoming feasible. Increasingly constructions

purely formed by bending can be replaced by more efficient tension constructions.
6 In former times, craftsmanship determined the quality in traditional building methods as a result of acquired human skill, today the perfection and speed of digital processes open up almost unlimited creative possibilities. For example CNC mills achieve the quality of something produced by a craftsman, but in doing this are significantly quicker and more precise.
7 The design, planning and construction of a project only take up a very slight proportion of the total life span of a building.
8 The duties of the architect have become more extensive.

2

3

With the aid of digital techniques it is possible to set objectives as early as in the design stage and then adapt and realize them. Through this procedure it is possible to anticipate deliverables effectively. Possible alterations can be simulated digitally and be quantified realistically in context.

As a result of these changed demands on design, the general aim to constantly generate as meaningful and verifiable data as possible, to interlink these data dynamically and to use them for guidance, is understandable. Similar developments are taking place in other sectors: new cars, for example, are not only supposed to operate more reliably, but they are also supposed to fit into the structures of our lives quietly, safely and without colliding, almost like in a shoal of fish. However, whilst cars and other consumer goods were able to make use of the benefits of industrial production through their manufacture in extensive numbers of units, building construction has always been at a disadvantage due to rarely achieving the status of series production, because generally buildings were one of a kind. With digital working processes this can change, which we can see from the example of another sector, namely the textile industry. Following the introduction of clothes fashion according to year and season, today mass customization, particularly in manufacturing, is an option for increasing production margins and developing new markets. However, mass customization and highly individualized execution only become possible with digital working processes and methods. In this publication we demonstrate to the architect who is involved in planning processes that the efficiency levels of other construction branches, such as automotive construction or product design, can be achieved.

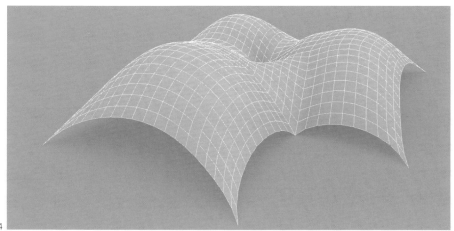

4

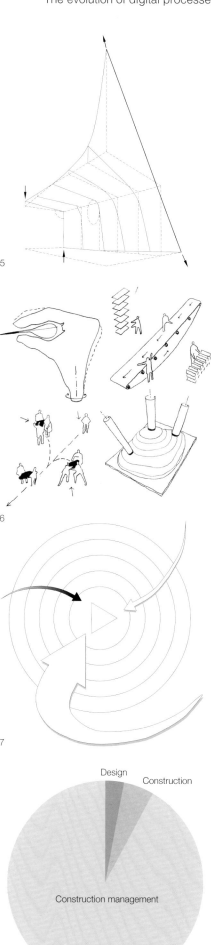

5

6

7

Design   Construction

Construction management

8

For the planner this provides the opportunity to open up other areas of responsibility, amongst others, data capture, evaluation of these data, optimization of solutions, and the simulation of planned results. Such further specializations will increasingly replace the old picture of the central master builder completely. It will only still be possible to work in a team in order to achieve holistic and sustainable overall solutions. At the same time, the risk of a superficial and faddish design resulting does not necessarily have to increase if all the technologies available are understood as being opportunities for new, contemporary solutions which are confidently implemented. And here plenty of knowledge, experience, talent, courage and hard work are needed. In particular questions about cost-effectiveness and liability will in the future, hopefully, allow for sustainable planning concepts. Economy and ecology should meld into one single requirement.

This book is intended to give an overview of digital techniques and of ways of working which make the day-to-day job of the planner easier and provide new possible solutions. As the Detail Practice series does not set itself out to be a comprehensive encyclopedia with exact "recipes" but rather is based upon a deliberately individual selection, certain important basic principles are tackled to aid better understanding and stimulate readers. As with the other books in the series the idea is that this book is fundamentally not about a particular style or trend. It is not about "blob" architecture or "smooth boxes" but rather about a better understanding of current possibilities from conception through to implementation, from the start to the finish of a building, or about the question of overall balance in the life cycle. As, in the future, there will be much more data on possible objec-

tives, results and deliverables, BIM (Building Information Model) software packages will link up designers, manufacturers and users comprehensively with one another. In the ideal scenario a BIM simulates the life cycle of a building before implementation and allows a building performance analysis to be carried out. As such, the efforts of individual specialists can grow to build a single pool of data which people can work on at different levels without loss, regardless of time or location. Working like this in digital project rooms, as is described in this book, must run smoothly from start to finish and correspond to digital levels of precision. However, the aesthetic design would need to be the result of careful individual decisions. As a general rule, "ingenious" solutions, proceeding by the trial and error method, or surprises at the implementation stage are to be avoided.

Konrad Wachsmann postulated grids and modules for intelligent planning and production in the 20th century. The resulting designs were determined by the desire for closed systems and series production. Today, however, technology opens up new possibilities for planners: thus in designing with digital methods we could, for example, do away with the compulsion for right angles. Comparable to developments in the Baroque or Rococo, two epochs which freed themselves from the compulsions of form and colour in a life-affirming way and as a result showed levels of joie de vivre not yet seen, there are new possibilities to be exploited. Even the complex ratios of the Golden Section should no longer cause problems, as they can be automatically calculated and implemented.

Well-proportioned solutions could be created in this way and harmonies in nature could give us cause to investigate and

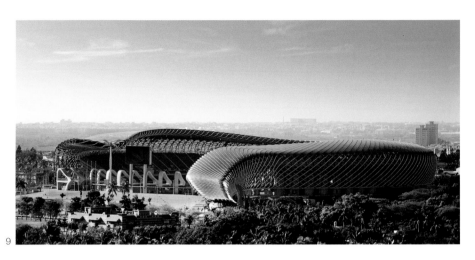

9

use age-old relationships and optimizations in the natural world for construction purposes. With today's digital methods this is possible at a fundamental level if we have the courage to operate in an innovative and responsible way. As the financial investments in hardware needed are also getting smaller and smaller, and as unrestricted "open source" and "cloud-based" working – so-called cloud computing – will become more and more straightforward, we can concentrate on the important thing – sustainable planning. Perhaps it will become clear from the selection of current real life examples that, alongside all the technology, a sense of what is beautiful can also show the way to what is correct and intelligible in architecture.

The second main section of this book is dedicated to the topic of production, as the digital planning methods described are complemented by innovations in the downstream production chain, prefabrication and construction implementation. The overarching goal is the establishment of a continuous digital chain [1], which creates a connection of all the incremental steps of the construction process without redundancies. Digital production technologies can be divided into three types: generative, subtractive, and transformative. Manufacturing procedures are analyzed example by example and visualized using reference objects. Subtractive and transformative procedures have been numerically controlled for 25 years, but every year the capability and simplicity of the control process increase. In the long term, the largest potential for digital production technologies lies in the additive procedures. With regard to architecture, in general, these technologies are still at the beginning of their development, in the medium term, however, they could contribute to the biggest revolution in design types.

Finally, in the last section of the book, six projects are showcased, whose complexity required the use of digital processes; something which has left its mark on them each in a different way. For example, an intelligent programmed algorithm generated the support structure of a pedestrian bridge in Reden and the so-called Sphere for the new headquarters of Deutsche Bank. This algorithm describes an iterative approximation process which eventually leads to the best and, as such, most efficient support structure solution. A human being would need forever for this gradual optimization process and for this reason would favour simple, obviously efficient solutions. In the past, constructing engineers like Félix Candela and Eladio Dieste have proven that efficiency and beauty are very closely related. A sensibly programmed computer can open up a new, and in general also aesthetically convincing, range of solutions.

The Hungerburg funicular railway demonstrates the use of project-specific special solutions for constructing a geometrically complex façade. Only through the variability of the software could the geometric variance of the curved glass façade be captured, efficiently planned and implemented.
The three projects – the National Temple of Divine Providence in Warsaw, the Rolex Learning Center in Lausanne, and the Taichung Metropolitan Opera House – are highly complex concrete-shell support structures, each demonstrating a different aspect of digital construction planning or construction implementation.

In the case of the National Temple, the emphasis is on the implementation of the design idea using a digitally conceived

9   Solar roof area aligned according to an efficiency analysis, sports stadium in Kaohsiung (RC) 2009, Toyo Ito

and controlled concrete formwork and reinforcement. Without the aid of computers, a construction like this would no longer be economically tenable in the 21st century due to significantly increased labour costs.

The Learning Center in Lausanne developed a completely new type of building. In the development phase the architects used a permanent feedback link between the architectural design, the logic of the support structure and efficient construction implementation. They managed to retain the integrity of the radical concept even under difficult circumstances.

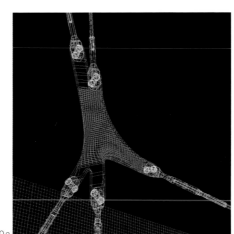

10a

The conceptual approach for the Tai-chung Metropolitan Opera House, which was originally developed manually, is translated into digital plans and models from which it is possible to draw conclusions for the design. Following this, the interdisciplinary work takes place using engineering specialists such as structural designers and acousticians, who introduce new parameters to the design. A permanent feedback link between all specialist disciplines determines the further development. Not least thanks to the digital methods established, the architect remains the integrating link in this design process. With the aid of digital processes the architect can succeed in preserving and reinforcing the original concept.

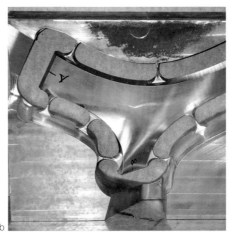

b

Notes:
[1] Schodek, Daniel: Digital Design and Manufacturing. CAD/CAM Applications in Architecture and Design. Hoboken 2005, p. 237ff.

10 Take Off, Munich Airport (D) 2003, Franken Architekten
    a Digitally modelled joint hub
    b CNC milled 3D joint hub
    c Mounted connection point

c

Digital planning technologies

Digital processes are continually increasing in importance in construction design. In contrast to the subjective and artistically formed way of thinking of architects, which is anchored in history, the new methods objectify the design process and create substantiated room for decision making. This chapter shows the broad-ranging spectrum of digital aids for planning, all of which require information on the location, the site and the geography to start with. Up until a few years ago these were all captured in individual plans and combined manually for each planning task. Today geo-data is available in real time. The data from geo-information systems (GIS) are linked into the planning process with direct interfaces and form an integral basis.

At the forefront, digital analysis techniques such as mapping, a data- and fact-based way of investigating the ground, are also in use. Using this, information is collated which previously would have had to be extracted with great effort and then transformed into usable planning data. Climatic data or movement diagrams, which are made up of complex sets of data, can, for example, be seamlessly integrated into the planning process. Differentiated simulations can help to optimize digital planning processes. Currently simulation software still mostly works uncoupled from the planning software. However, in the medium term you can count on these two planning levels growing together, which will allow real time simulations free of interfaces.

2D computer-aided design and computer-aided architectural design programs have been in existence since the beginning of the 1980s. Initially they enabled a better working procedure compared with working with the pencil. Since the 1990s, 3D CAAD software has been in use in architectural offices. In the beginning it was primarily used for visualizing spaces and constructions as well as for quantity surveying and visualization of construction procedures over time. At the beginning of the noughties, object-based (construction element related) design is finding its way into offices and is increasing the efficiency of the design process when working with repetitive elements. Today more and more so-called rule-based (parametric) software techniques are in use, whose programmed data models of architectural design processes open up numerous variation studies in a simple way. This process is also referred to as "generative design".

The efficiency of surveying is increased markedly through new methods. Photogrammetry and 3D laser scanning technology generate fully adequate sets of data of existing buildings which can then be supplemented by the continued design process. In offices such as Gehry and Partners a methodology involving feedback loops between analogue and digital models using 3D scanners has been developed.

In order to undertake projects efficiently it makes sense to have a digitally linked-up basis for project organization, such as the transparent project room described.

The fully integrated building information model is a compaction of CAAD software-based planning to a fully digital building model. It enables holistic building process organization which reaches from the design and construction stages through to facility management.

In the last part of the chapter the legal consequences, which result from using the new planning and manufacturing technologies, are illustrated.

1 Varying spatial structure, which was implemented in a completely computer-controlled way using CAD-CAM techniques.

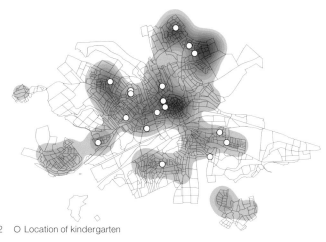

2   O Location of kindergarten

Building with poten-
tial for adding a floor
3   (FSI < 1)

Depiction of the
maximum options for
adding floors

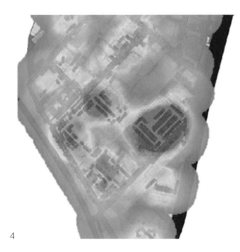

4

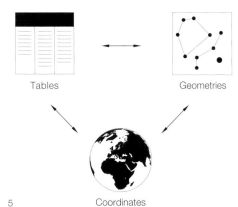

Tables

Geometries

5   Coordinates

Geographic information systems

The abbreviation GIS stands for "geo-graphic information system". A GIS is used for the capture, organization, processing, analysis, depiction and presentation of spatial information. The popular programs Google Earth or Bing Maps, which are freely accessible to a broad public, could be called "GIS", and it is difficult to imagine them not being used every day. However, neither of the programs named have any analysis or evaluation functions and they are not exact enough for professional use. A fully adequate GIS is a software program for depicting and processing spatial information in the form of maps, aerial shots, height models or technical data, which in addition can create images and effectively and meaningfully analyze quantitative and qualitative spatial contexts such as, for example, diagrams of shadows.

Data sources
Simply put, a GIS consists of a software environment and data which must be brought together by a service provider. It is not uncommon for people to think that all the information would be already contained in a GIS just like with Google Earth. However, for each project, relevant, appropriate and available data must first of all be obtained. There are various data sources for this:
· Commercial providers
· Specialist authorities and departments, planning and statistics offices
· Web services
· Data generated or gathered oneself

These sources provide a variety of data and map material which can be embedded straight into the GIS.

Set-up and functionality
In a GIS there are clearly located (geo-referenced) geometry data such as points, lines or surfaces linked to technical data (attributes). Geometric information such as, for example, the surface of an area of land can be visually represented, described and evaluated based on attributes like the size of the area of land, owner, usage etc. Furthermore, situation-based analyses can be carried out in order to determine the distance of objects from one another. Alongside these technical and location-based queries the GIS can also provide topological evaluations which affect the spatial relationships between the individual objects – e.g. that object A is located within object B or A and B share a line segment. Complex spatial analyses which combine, blend or offset various types of information are also possible (e.g. density analysis, spatial statistics and much more). Vector and grid data, tables and databases such as, for example, the factors involved when searching for a location for a central multi-storey car park in a business park which can be reached by the majority of staff in the shortest time possible, can be entered into the GIS, processed and displayed (fig. 4). There are many interface and interchange possibilities with other applications such as, for example, CAD or simulation programs and formats; when carrying out a space utilization analysis, for example, route data of selected target groups can be recorded with GPS devices, attributed with specific information and evaluated.

2   Population density analysis of the age group of 0–3 year olds in order to establish suitable locations for kindergartens (the darker the shade the more residents)
3   Calculation of re-densification potential or potential for adding floors
4   Establishing a suitable location for a multi-storey car park in a commercial area. Condition: must be quick to reach for as many employees as possible
5   Information levels of a GIS

6

Benefits for architects and planners
Most departments who record data now generate and disseminate all relevant basic data such as cadastral maps, land registry data, terrain models or orthophotos originally in a GIS-based form.

Architects and planners can input these data very easily and without time-consuming conversion into a GIS and use them immediately. As a result of the clear geo-reference all the data are in the correct position and even project data, perhaps from a CAD program, can be loaded in the right position. So, for example, the calculation of redensification potential can be carried out based on land registry data via the attributes floor area, number of floors, and plot area. Furthermore, GIS are able to generate clearly legible maps or plan documents from data relevant to the situation, which reproduce spatial contexts in a pictorial

and understandable form. This is why they are suited to being used by architects and planners particularly on all projects where the processing of extensive spatial data material is necessary. In doing this, it is possible to combine completely different themes and objects with the aid of spatial reference, in order to make urban or spatial qualities and functionalities easier to interpret and to make decision-making processes more transparent, more efficient and clearer. Fields of use here are, above all, analyses of complex circumstances surrounding construction and planning projects, location analyses and evaluations. In addition, GIS are used in the simulation of existing or future spatial developments, as is the case, for example, in the planning of kindergarten requirements for a whole municipal area using population density analysis (fig. 2).

Martin Berchtold, Philipp Krass

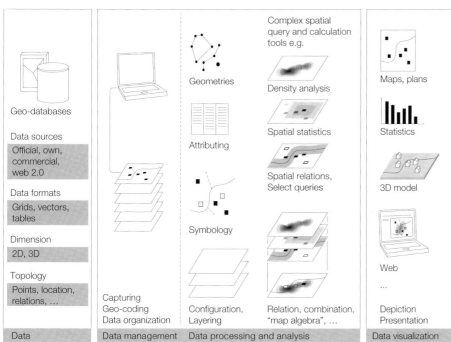

7

6 Spatial usage analysis, depiction of the routes covered (according to mode of transport) and locations (according to reason for visit)
7 Graphical representation of the interdependencies of a GIS structure.

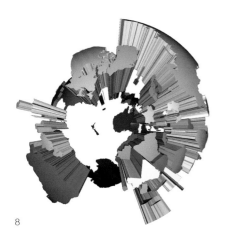

8

8 MobiGlobe, Autostadt Wolfsburg, media installation about automobility. The research project uses
   interactive three dimensional graphics in order to
   underlay topics such as the "autobahn town" or
   the "oil world" with critical information.
9 Visualization of a statistical analysis of incidents
   relating to individual areas of the town

10 Flow map; the layout is the result of program-
    ming.
11 Diagram of an infrastructure system as well
    as the transformation of the associated spatial
    program into an architectonic structure
12 Analysis and visual depiction of the commuter re-
    gions of Switzerland and their economic power.

Analysis techniques – Mapping

Definition of the term / usage
The term "mapping" describes the preparation and visualization of information
at a numerical, notational and graphical
level. Maps incorporate large amounts
of data in a compact information design
which makes it possible for the user to
read it quickly. Planning maps, picto-
grams, symbols and overarching relational depictions unify various types of
representation and scales in a single
graphical image (fig. 9). The demands
when deciphering these relational maps

grow with the complexity of the data
depicted.
The architect can use maps to prepare
information in a compact form and as a
result give all interest groups involved in
the planning process room to make decisions. A parametric linkage of the data
used enables the user to graphically simulate and evaluate them and, as a result,
clarify objective setting. Mapping extends
the usual methods of depicting plans
such as:
• Flow maps (fig. 10)
• Statistical GIS maps
• Conceptual and mind maps

• Network maps
• Radial maps

Overall, with this selection of mapping
methods, you can differentiate between
the following types of visualization: process visualizations (temporary sequences)
or structural visualizations (hierarchies or
networks), which depict either creative or
analytical thought processes in varying
degrees of detail.

Data collection
The basis for mapping is either data
which you have collected yourself or data

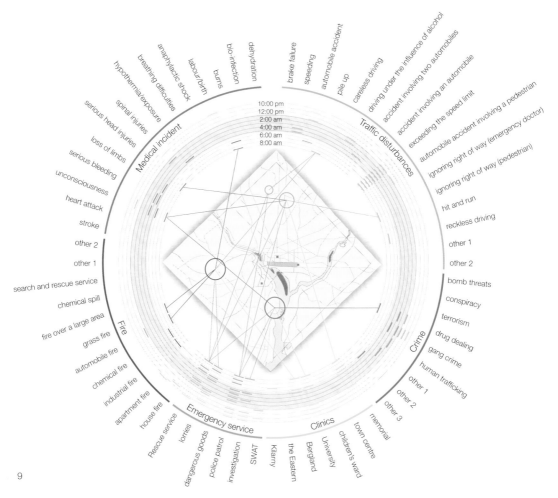

9

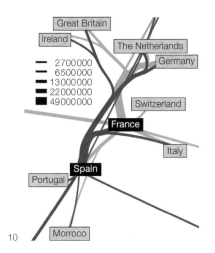

10

Escalator
Diagonal upwards
movement

Stairs
Diagonal upwards
and downwards
movement

Lift
Vertical upwards
and downwards
movement

11

sourced from external providers. As part of this process, topographical, spatial and surface-related, geometric, social and consumer statistical, physical or chemical data can be used. These can be sourced from both public authorities such as offices for statistics and local councils as well as from commercial data providers.

Methods
Qualitative visualizations such as network diagrams (Fuzzy Cognitive Maps) and conceptual maps are used to document planning goals, discussions and work-

shops in order to establish spatial allocation plans for the design. These methods are also suitable for the dynamic development of room books. FCMs mostly use two-dimensional relations of selected groups or concepts together, comparable with the locations and routes of a map. The priority setting takes place using the attachment strength of social units and the importance of information flows in an initially diffuse spatial organization. In an urban construction context FCMs visualize the relations of the interest groups with one another as well as with the town planning institutions

through degrees of proximity. Based on formal models of concepts and their relational qualities (semantic networks) conceptual maps bundle the results of a planning-specific collection of knowledge or ideas (brainstorming) in a precise, logically linked order. This method for producing checklists and protocols accommodates the human thought process through its non-linearity, as it allows for additions and alterations to be made.

The digital linking of concepts, sketches and images allows for a comprehensive

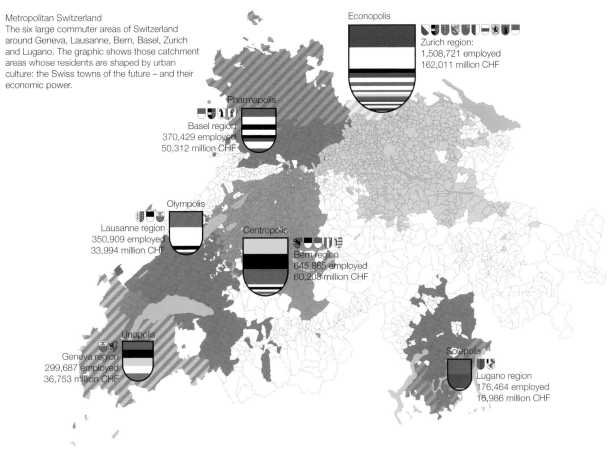

Metropolitan Switzerland
The six large commuter areas of Switzerland around Geneva, Lausanne, Bern, Basel, Zurich and Lugano. The graphic shows those catchment areas whose residents are shaped by urban culture: the Swiss towns of the future – and their economic power.

Econopolis
Zurich region:
1,508,721 employed
162,011 million CHF

Pharmapolis
Basel region
370,429 employed
50,312 million CHF

Olympolis
Lausanne region
350,909 employed
33,994 million CHF

Centropolis
Bern region
645,865 employed
60,208 million CHF

Unopolis
Geneva region
299,687 employed
36,753 million CHF

Solepolis
Lugano region
176,464 employed
16,986 million CHF

12

13

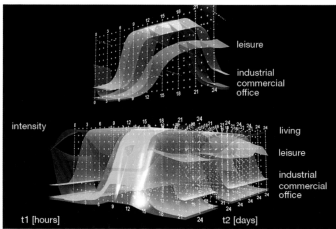

leisure

industrial
commercial
office

intensity

living

leisure

industrial
commercial
office

t1 [hours]   t2 [days]

14

itemization of knowledge. Mind maps lend themselves to visualizations of purely knowledge-based structures. However, the topics represented in different thought categories should only demonstrate remote relations between the various branches of the tree structure, as otherwise both the clarity and general validity for third parties are lost. The direct transfer of mapping into the design process can be read off during so-called diagrammatic designing. This method uses the abstract depiction of spatial contexts in the form of maps (e.g. traffic flow in a building) in order to establish foundations for certain architectural decisions.

The most promising potential of mapping for society is in interactive, digital collection processes, which enable a real-time analysis of municipal and building engineering planning parameters. Behavioural and usage patterns of interest groups can be captured using digital town mapping techniques (data mining processes). GPS positioning technology, in combination with portable mobile devices, also simplifies considerably the amount of personnel required for field research methods to record urban construction processes (fig. 13). This method, which has been

technically possible since 2008, must, however, be secured in terms of data protection law and requires the prior permission of all involved.

Vision
On the Semantic Web, a network equipped with interpretative intelligence which is still in development, information from various sources can be partly automated and linked to form new document series via the Internet. The planned high-speed Internet infrastructure will aid digitally transparent planning procedures (see "project room", p. 29ff) as well as user-friendly online simulations. The methods described offer planners the possibility of capturing and depicting the parameters of each project phase in a compact form. Through the integration of substantiated sets of data, mapping can become a means of communication between interest groups and planners or even the medium of a political process. Planners are called upon to forecast, follow up and verify usage and development-specific aspects of their planning. Simulatively linked planning processes optimize planning and as such can lead to broad backing from the community.

Simulation and optimization

Definition/benefits
Like mapping, simulation uses algorithms for preparing and processing information. With simulation procedures, complex systems and processes, such as flow behaviours, can be imitated in their progression, which is in most cases dynamic. Here we distinguish between virtual (software-based) simulation, such as finite element calculation, and physical (model-based) simulation, such as chain models. Both simulation methods deliver fact-based insights into the form and structure of a design and thereby reinforce the planning safety in building construction and town planning. As physical simulation is much more resource-intensive than virtual simulation, the software industry is trying to simulate reality as exactly as possible by means of their programs in order to save time and costs. The following contribution highlights the potential of virtual simulation. Hardware which is faster and faster and software which is easier and easier to use open up a wealth of simulation fields such as:
· Acoustic simulation
· Fire behaviour simulation

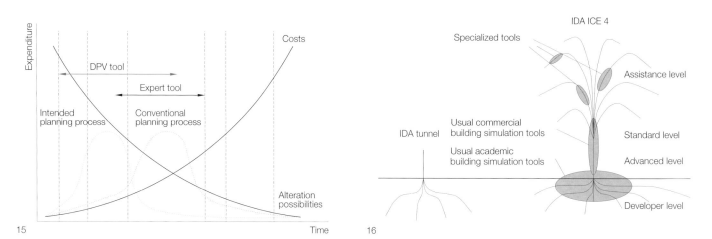

15   Time   16

17

- Energy efficiency simulation
- Light simulation
- Ventilation/air flow simulation (fig. 17)
- Spatial usage simulation
- Static simulation (frame programs and finite element programs)
- Thermal simulation (fig. 21, p. 20)
- Traffic flow simulation

Database for simulation
Similar to mapping, simulation software requires precise base data. The user can either establish these values themselves or take them from corresponding parameter databases for the simulation exercise in hand. In order to create dynamic building simulations, data from the energy, water and communications industries as well as statistical data from public institutions are used. For example, the EnEV (DIN 18599 "Energetic Evaluation of Buildings") defines the basic data requirements for a simulation of heating requirements. Software such as IDA ICE supports the user through intelligently structured, easy-to-use user interfaces and input masks (fig. 16), which reduce the effort required for inputting. This helps avoid redundancies and supports the early use of data in the design.

Interactive simulations not only set inputted values in relation to the planning object, but also lead to fact-based, digital form finding and structuring in the design process. In the medium term, planning and simulation environments will grow together. Currently the interface is bridged using graphical scripting tools, which are explained in the chapter "The use of programming in architecture" (p. 24ff). A real-time use of algorithms, for example, as integrated into the Kangaroo software by Daniel Piker, supports interactive geometric alterations. With this dynamic simulation software it is possible to more specifically define the as yet manual calculations of specialist planners involved.

Use
The visualization of three-dimensional forms with textures and lighting situations as a spatial simulation has been standard architectural design practice for many years. The same volumetric data model is the basis for the simulation software solutions used by specialist planners as described in the following.

A central field of simulation application is the structural-building physics optimization of constructions using structural-mechanical calculations with FEM software (Finite Element Method). Through the use of software such as Abaqus or Ansys, engineering firms are able to simulate complex constructions which were difficult to capture with classical bar framework methods, and optimize them step by step. Air flow simulations (computer fluid dynamics) are supplemented with location-specific environmental factors and as such improve the basic static assumptions. For example, in this way, the geometry of a restaurant on a mountain (fig. 18) can be optimally shaped with regard to the anticipated wind load resistance.

In developing new material systems or building components so-called multiphysics simulation programs are used, which examine thermo-structural interdependencies (fig. 19) of different materials. As part of a research project at the Technical University in Darmstadt the reverse expansion coefficient of carbon fibre reinforced plastic (CRP) and polyvinyl chloride (PVC) were simulated in the Comsol

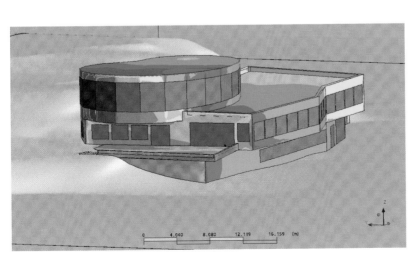

18

13 "Seven Year Drawing", routes covered in Berlin between 2003 and 2009, recorded using GPS tracking
14 Diagram of a programmatic town district activity pattern
15 Opportunities for the early use of simulation software
16 Usage and functionality levels of simulation software using IDA ICE4 as an example
17 Flow simulation on a restaurant on the Hoher Kasten mountain in St. Gallen (CH)
18 Simulation of the stagnation pressure on the restaurant

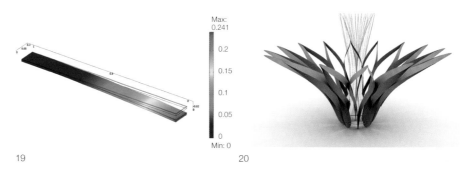

19 20

software. For this purpose, the geometry of a building component with two different material components is modelled on the computer and connected with the material parameters made available in the program, such as the heat expansion coefficient. Finally, the program simulates an increase in the ambient temperature by, for example, 20 degrees Celsius. The modelled components show a dynamic distortion which can be captured exactly. The physical prototypes, which were subsequently prepared in the workshops of the Technical University in Darmstadt, confirmed the results of the virtual prototype.

Conclusion
The use of simulation at an early stage helps to avoid structural weaknesses in the course of the design phase (fig. 15, p. 18). At the beginning of a project, for example, the potentially cost-relevant factors, such as the span of beams, are defined and used as the basis for the simulation as concrete parameters. In this way you can create an instrument for early cost control. Typically the ideal goal of virtual simulation technology is an anticipated life cycle analysis of the building under examination, which, for example, allows energy consumption over the next 20 years in varying usage scenarios to be captured.

Of most use for the future are those simulation solutions which can be utilized in such an uncomplicated way that it is not only experts who are capable to work with them. In the future there will be a closer and closer linkage of planning

Below 42.95 °C	50.57 to 54.38 °C	62.01 to 65.82 °C	Over 73.44 °C
42.95 to 46.76 °C	54.38 to 58.20 °C	65.82 to 69.63 °C	Min: 39.14 °C
46.76 to 50.57 °C	58.20 to 62.01 °C	69.63 to 73.44 °C	Max: 77.25 °C

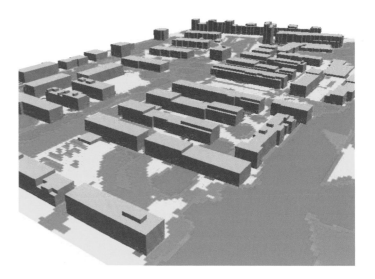

21

software with simulation software. This is why the correct interpretation of simulation results is becoming a key qualification for future planners and designers.

19 Simulation of a material system consisting of CRP and PVC in the Comsol software
20 Thermo-dynamic expansive structure based on a material system consisting of CRP and GRP
21 Simulation of the Physiologically Equivalent Temperature (PET) of the municipal district of Freiburg-Vauban
22 Itemization of the planning instruments against the complexity of the task

Computer-aided architectural design (CAAD)

Since the middle of the 1980s, architectural firms have been using CAAD. As part of this process, planning documents are generated with the aid of special software, which can be further categorized as 2D, 2 ½ D, and 3D CAD programs.

2D CAD systems are primarily an extension of the drafting board – the method is the same, just using a different tool. All drawing elements follow the vector-based configuration system of point, line, polylines, arcs, splines and planes. The organization of drawings using levels and symbols along with the logical linkages between individual drawing elements increase the efficiency. Through so-called plug-ins, small software add-ons, the

functionality can be extended or adapted in a user-specific way.

With 2 ½ D programs we are dealing with simulated 3D technology, where the user can opt to use 3D objects within a 2D drawing level. These building elements such as walls, ceilings, windows etc. are either provided by the program to choose from in a library, or the user can import them from various manufacturers. As its basic logic is easy to understand, this type of program is used in a large number of planning offices, above all for projects with a manageable level of complexity. However, there is the danger that these programs encourage a certain characteristic architectonic style and therefore result in less varied designs. 3D software becomes necessary as soon

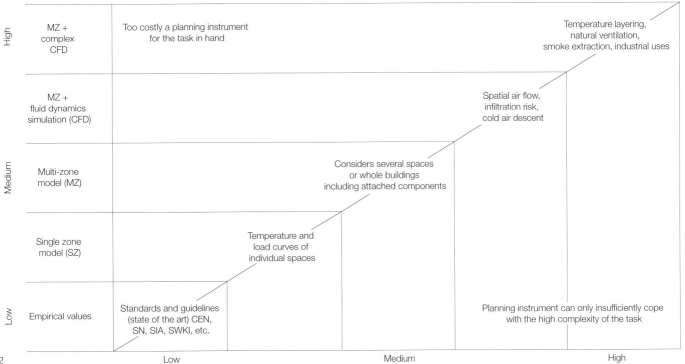

Itemization grade of the planning instruments

Optimal planning instrument for performing the task

High — MZ + complex CFD
Too costly a planning instrument for the task in hand
Temperature layering, natural ventilation, smoke extraction, industrial uses

MZ + fluid dynamics simulation (CFD)
Spatial air flow, infiltration risk, cold air descent

Medium — Multi-zone model (MZ)
Considers several spaces or whole buildings including attached components

Single zone model (SZ)
Temperature and load curves of individual spaces

Low — Empirical values
Standards and guidelines (state of the art) CEN, SN, SIA, SWKI, etc.
Planning instrument can only insufficiently cope with the high complexity of the task

22

Low   Medium   High

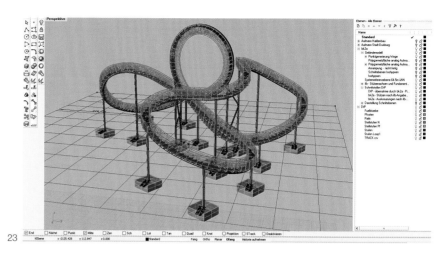

23

as the architect is working with multiple curved surfaces with varying curve geometry or dynamic structures. The programs mostly originate from fields such as product design and automobile construction and have been adapted to the needs of and specially developed for architecture since the middle of the 1990s. The software offers the designer a great freedom to model geometries and to modify them via a variety of operators (program-specific software options). As an extension to this, parametric 3D software enables the associative linkage of virtual building elements and thus the intelligent structuring of planning processes. The programming of so-called plug-ins or scripts (project-specific software add-ons) allows specific functions such as, for example, the gradual alteration of a beam cross-section in relation to the loading condition. The interactive linkage, for example, with supporting structure planning software, enables a feedback loop, which as early as in the planning phase makes a contribution to the optimization of the project. Important deciding factors when buying a product are, amongst other things, geometry options, BIM connection, AVA (tender – contract awarding – invoicing) connection and variety of the integrated interfaces

(table T1). Most software packages require extensive knowledge in order to make use of the full potential of the program. The planner should avoid frequently switching between individual software systems.

The future of digital construction planning lies in the close linkage of the software of all specialist planning disciplines involved; for this a smooth flow of data via a standardized interface is a fundamental requirement. Up until now, however, software manufacturers have not been able to agree on a uniform exchange format which bundles all of the information. Since the middle of the 1990s the dxf/dwg format has become the standard used in all programs, which allows 2D exchange of information. With companies such as metal and timber construction companies, whose production is computer-controlled (see chapter "Production technologies"), the direct transfer of the planning data into the production data is already possible.

Since 1999 the manufacturer-independent universal IFC format (Industry Foundation Class) has been under development. It transfers information on building

components which extend beyond pure geometry, such as mass, material, costs etc. This interface eliminates incompatibilities and mistakes in the transfer of digital information and leads to a significant increase in efficiency. It is being developed by a non-commercial consortium of software manufacturers, architects and construction companies into an industry standard.
Provided the Industry Foundation Class develops into a standard like the dxf/dwg format it will result in a continuous linkage or interaction with upstream (specialist planners) and downstream (AVA – tender – contract awarding – invoicing/facility management) software. In the interim, various software houses have already created individual interfaces for connecting to AVA software, but with it the user always has to go for a more extensive software package. IFC enables an individual interconnection of the software required for each planning task.

23 Integral CAD model of the walk-in sculpture Angerpark Landmark, Duisburg
24 Angerpark Landmark, example of isometry of the varying flight of steps
25 Angerpark Landmark, parametric variance of the cross-beams

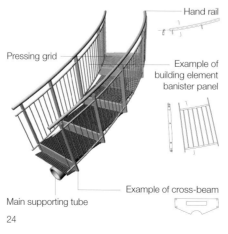

24

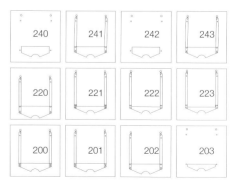

25

T1: comparison of common architecture software

Software	Extensions and plug-ins	Operating systems	Primary application	2D/3D	Geometry bases	Object-based	BIM	Parametrics	Memory format	Interface format	Commercial/student version [€]
Alias Sketch/ Sketchbook Pro (2004)	Plug-ins and add-ons	Windows/ Mac OS	Concept design/ set design/illustrations/ storyboarding	•/-	2D pixel graphics	-	-	None	ai	Image formats	179/0
Illustrator (1987)	Application-related plug-ins/add-ons	Windows/ Mac OS	Illustrations	*/-	2D vector graphics	-	-	None	ai	ai, dxf, dwg, eps, fxg, pdf, svg, swf, Image formats	599/199 [$]
Corel Draw (1989)	Application-related plug-ins/add-ons	Windows	Illustrations	*/-	2D vector graphics	-	-	None	cdr	ai, cgm, docx, dwg, dxf, pdf, psd, raw, Image formats	630/99
Inkscape (2003)	Application-related extensions	Windows/ Mac OS/ Linux	Illustrations	*/-	2D vector graphics	-	-	None	svg/ pdf	dxf, Image formats	0/0
Auto CAD (Architecture) (1982)	Architecture including 3D building component library, Speedikon	Windows/ (Linux)	All planning phases/ 3D visualization	*/*	(Poly)lines, circles, arcs, splines, surface, network and volume modelling as a volume edge representation	(•)	•	2D	dwg	3ds, adsk, dwf, dwfx, dwg, dws, dwt, dxb, dxf, dxx, ifc, LandXML, mdb, mwx, pdf, plt, sdf	1189/0
Allplan Architecture (1984)	BCM, planning data, Allfa	Windows	All planning phases/ D visualization	*/*	As before, linked surface fillings	•	•	Building component	ndw	dwg, dxf, 3ds, a4d, c4u, ifc, wrl, u3d, 3dm, 3ds, skp, ifc, iges	1495/0
ArchiCAD (1984)	EcoDesigner, TeamBuilding	Windows/ Mac OS	All planning phases/ 3D visualization	*/*	As before, linked surface fillings	•	•	Building component	pln	3ds, atl, c4d, dgn, dwg, dwf, dxf, eps, epx, fact, ifc, ifcxml, lp, obj, pdf, plt, sat, sgi, skp, u3d, wrl, image and mixed formats	2950/0
Microstation (1985)	Bentley Architecture, Speedikon, Generative Components (2003)	Windows	All planning phases/ 3D visualization	*/*	As before, linked surface fillings	•	•	2D	dgn	3dm, dwg, dxf, gbxml, ifc, iges, pdf, rvt, skg, stl, step, u3d, x_t	7378/95
VectorWorks Architecture (1985)	Interior design, urban and landscape planning	Windows/ Mac OS	All planning phases/ 3D visualization	*/*	As before, linked surface fillings	•	•	Building component	vwx	3ds, atl, dxf, dwg, epsf, hdri, ifc, iges, kml, pdf, sat, shape, skp, stl, x_t, Image formats	4450/0
FormZ (1991)	Plug-ins	Windows/ Mac OS	3D modelling/ 3D visualization	*/*	As before, only better surface/ volume modelling	(•)	•	•	fmz	ai, atl, dae, dem, dwg, dxf, eps, epx, fact, iges, kmz, lw, lp, obj, pdf, plt, ib, sat, skg, step, stl, zpr, Image formats	1049/32
Rhino (1992)	Grasshopper (2007), VisualArq, Rhiknowbot, Rhinoparametrics, further plug-ins	Windows/ (Mac OS)	All planning phases/ 3D construction development/Parameterization of complex geometries/ 3D visualization	*/*	As before, only better surface/ volume modelling	(•)	(•)	(•)	3dm, ghx	3dm, 3ds, ai, dwg, dxf, iges, step, sat, VDA, x_t, obj, pov, raw, rib, stl, udo, VRML, wmf, DirectX, csv/txt, slc, zpr, GHS, WAMIT, fbx, XGL, cd, lwo, kml, ply	1184/232 / Grasshopper 0/0
Revit Architecture (1999)	Plug-ins/add-ons e.g. D-A-CH for calculations	Windows	All planning phases/3D visualization	(*)/*	As before	•	•	•	rvt	rvt, dwg, dwf, dxf, 3ds, ifc, dgn, sat, gbXML	5500/0
SketchUp (2000)	Lots of plug-ins and ruby scripts	Windows/ Mac OS	Up to design planning/3D sketches + modelling + visualization	*/*	As before, simple surface/volume modelling	•	(•)	(•)	skp	3ds, dae, dem, ddf, dwg, dxf, eps, epx, fbx, kmz, obj, pdf, vrml, wrl, xsi, Image formats	0–373
bonzai3d (2009)		Windows/ Mac OS	All planning phases/ 3D sketches + modelling + visualization	*/*	As before, only better surface/volume modelling	•	-	Objects	bnz	3ds, ai, atl, dwg, dxf, eps, epx, kmz, lwo, obj, psd, qt, sat, w3d, stl, Image formats	459 €/40 $
3D Max Design (1990)	Lots of plug-ins	Windows/ (Mac OS)	3D visualization/ animation	-/*	As before, only better surface/network/volume modelling	•	-	(•)	3ds	ai, asc, ase, dwg, dxf, fbx, iges, obj, prj, sat, shp, skp, stl, wrl, wrz, film and image formats	4641/148
Cinema 4D (1993)	Lots of plug-ins	Windows/ Mac OS/ Linux	3D visualization/ animation	-/*	As before, only better surface/network/volume modelling	•	-	(•)	C4d	3dmf, 3ds, ai, bva, bvh, dae, dem, dwg, dxf, eps, fbx, iges, lw, mon, ndw, obj, pln, rib, rpc, stl, swf, vwx, wrl, wrz, 25 formats via Polytrans	1500/96
Houdini (1996)	Plug-ins	Windows/ Mac OS	3D visualization/ animation	-/*	As before, only better surface/network/volume modelling	•	-	•	geo/ bgeo	dxf, eps, iv, lw, med, obj, pc, ply, poly, rib, sdl, wrl, Image formats	1195/6995 [$]
Blender (1998)	Plug-ins	Windows/ Mac OS/ Linux	3D visualization/ animation	-/*	As before, only better surface/network/volume modelling	•	-	(•)	blend	3ds, ac, dae, eps, fig, flt, dec, lwo, map, md2, mot, ms3d, obj, dxf, ps, slp, stl, svg, vrml, x3d, xsi	0
Maya (1998)	Lots of plug-ins	Windows/ Mac OS/ Linux	3D visualization/ animation	-/*	As before, only better surface/network/volume modelling	•	-	(•)	ma/mb	ai, dxf, eps, fbx, flt, ge2, iges, iv, mel, obj, ps, rib, rtg, wire, wrl, wrz, svg, swf, t3m, film and image formats	3495/166,60
City Engine (2007)	-	Windows/ Mac OS/ Linux	3D modelling/town growth simulation	-/*	As before, quick geometry generation (Shape Grammar)	•	-	•	cej/ cga	3ds, dae, dxf, fbx, mas, ml, osm, rib, obj, shp, Image formats	495–4950/ 149 [$]
UGS NX (1981)	Add-ons and plug-ins	Windows/ Mac OSX/ Linux/Unix	Automotive/mechanical engineering/industrial design	(*)/*	As before, but real volume modelling	•	-	•	ug	asm, ca4, cat, dwg, dxf, iges, jt, mf1, step, sw, stl, x_t	8000+/199
Catia (1982)	Digital Project, Primavera, Imagine & Shape, Photo Studio	Windows/ Unix/ Solaris	Architecture/mechanical engineering/aviation	(*)/*	As before, but real volume modelling	•	•	•	catpart/ catproduct	3dxml, cgm, csv, dwg, dxf, iges, pdf, plt, step, stl, vrml, xls	10000+/75 o. Digital Project 17000+ $/ 180 p.a.
Alias (1985)	Part components Design, Surface & Automotive	Windows/ Mac OS	Automotive/mechanical engineering/industrial design	(*)/*	As before, hybrid surface and network modelling, sketching	•	-	-	wire	dxf, dwf, iges, step, catia, ugs nx, prt/asm, ptc granite, jt, slddrw, Image formats	4000–89000/ 0 [$]
ProEngineer (1989)	Lots of special attachments	Windows/ Solaris	mechanical engineering/ industrial design	(*)/*	As before, but real volume modeling	•	-	•	prt/ asm	dxf, iges, step, set, vda, ecad, cgm, cosmos/m, patran, supertab, sla, render, vrml	6850–34200/99
CoCreate (1995)	Lots of special attachments	Windows	mechanical engineering/ industrial design	(*)/*	As before, dynamic modelling	•	-	(•)	pkg	cat, dwg, dxf, iges, pcb, pdf, olt, ps, sat, slddrw, step, stl, ug, x_t, vrml ...	0–3170 p.a.
Solid Works (1996)		Windows	mechanical engineering/ industrial design	(*)/*	As before, but real volume modelling	•	-	•	Slddrw	dxf, dwg, Parasolid, iges, step, acis, stl, u3d, vrml, 3dxml, catia	9995/99

23

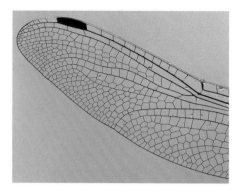

26

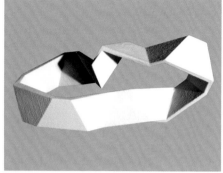

27

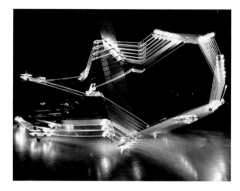

28

Rule-based planning – parametrics

Nature seldom operates with orthogonal systems. It selects efficient, material-optimized solutions. A dragonfly's wing, for example, demonstrates the use of a load-specific structural system, which has developed in an evolutionary process (fig. 26). In contrast, for reasons of efficiency, engineers in construction work primarily with right-angled systems, which in many cases results in redundancies. Digital planning and production today offer the potential of specific solution variations which lead to new structural forms in architecture. Parametric planning methods are the digital foundation for this.

In order to capture the potential of parametrics and its implementation strategies in architecture, we first of all need to define our terms. The term "parameter" comes from mathematics and is used across disciplines to describe factors which determine a series of variations. In construction the term mostly refers to concrete building parameters or environmental factors which provide particular limit parameters and variables.

As such, the relationships amongst and between all elements of a digital building model are defined in the parametrics software and set dependent on one another.

In this way alterations to the building model are possible while at the same time maintaining maximum consistency. For updating the drawings or linkages the user does not need to do anything; the software updates itself immediately with each alteration to each element. The linkage information, which is captured during the conception of the parametric model, forms the basis for this.

Heike Matcha

Use of programming in architecture
For a long time in architecture, programs have been set up which conceptually determine the design principles and in this way make design decisions possible. With the classic design process these programs are in most cases loosely defined or used unconsciously. However, if they are set up exactly, then clearly defined spaces open up for generating

variations and optimizations, which can be taken advantage of with the help of computer technology as part of a generative design process.

In practice, design principles like this can be represented using parametric models. Generally they are set up using existing CAD software with corresponding add-ons. An additional benefit is the direct access to existing data in the CAD formats and the possibility of flexibly controlling functions belonging to the program. Several CAD manufacturers offer various possibilities for interaction with their programs which vary in their capability and complexity.

Distinctions are made between scripting, the creation of smaller programs with comparatively simple programming languages, and real programming with more complex programming languages, but also significantly higher capability, such as, for example, directly controlling CNC machines.

This distinction is superimposed by the relatively new concept of visual programming such as the Grasshopper develop-

26 Wing of a dragonfly with gradated, load-adapted transition of cell structures
27 Study model of an exhibition stand in the form of a polygonal Moebius band
28 Realized exhibition stand based on a solution variation from the software Matlab, which was realized via a continuous digital chain
29 Geometric abstractions of the Moebius structure in the software Matlab

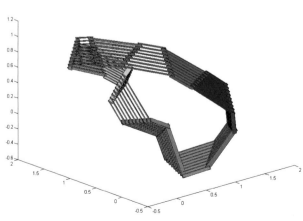

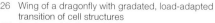

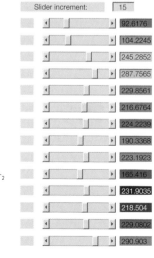

29

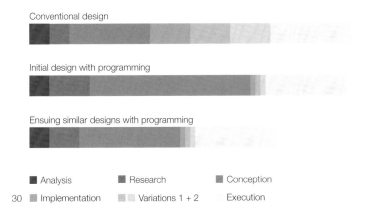

Conventional design

Initial design with programming

Ensuing similar designs with programming

■ Analysis　　　■ Research　　　■ Conception

30　■ Implementation　　■ Variations 1 + 2　　□ Execution

ment environment (fig. 31) provided for the CAD program Rhinoceros. Instead of a description in text form, here, predefined graphical components, which represent stages of processing, are linked with the mouse, which defines a logical construction sequence. Alterations to any point of this definition are directly transferred by the parametric linkages to all relevant points of the overall model. Once a logic circuit has been defined for a construction it can be used for various geometrical outcomes.

In order to make the working procedure and potential when designing with parametric models clearer, these are illustrated in the following example using the form structuring process by means of structural support analysis software. This design was created in the course of developing an entry for a competition to design a greenhouse in Bolzano.

A predetermined external building surface area served as the basis for the form structuring process, onto which possible positions for the steel substructure were parametrically defined using a Grasshopper script.

As the dimension of the steel cross-sections has a decisive influence on the visual appearance and the amount of shade the interior of the building has, this was automatically calculated via a structural analysis and transferred into the model. To do this the positions of the supports were first parametrically determined by dividing the external surface area and then were transmitted again via a programming interface to the structural support analysis program (fig. 36, p. 26). Alongside the purely structural data it was possible to determine areas of load application based on the division of the surface, and apply a predefined weight per unit area to the calculation model in the form of linear member loads. Through iterative calculation (fig. 32 and 33, p. 26) and adjustment the cross-section was then determined and subsequently transferred back to the parametric model. In this way it was possible to directly investigate the dimensioning of the building components and as such the visual appearance depending on the division of the surface area.

Despite the high degree of automation, those involved in the project selected the parameter sets to be investigated in a targeted way, and by this means manually limited the scope of the solutions. In the first instance this approach was selected in order to keep the time required for the task within an acceptable limit. In this way it was possible to do without calculating all possible parameter combinations and subsequently filtering hundreds of partly very similar, partly uneconomical solutions.

An approach like this is just one example of using programming. The spectrum of possibilities for use ranges from solving time-consuming tasks such as the automated layout of design plans, to directly extracting production data for CNC machines from 3D models, to logistical usages such as labelling building components with bar codes. What all

30　Design sub-processes; the focus of the design is on the conception of the process
31　Visual programming environment – Grasshopper

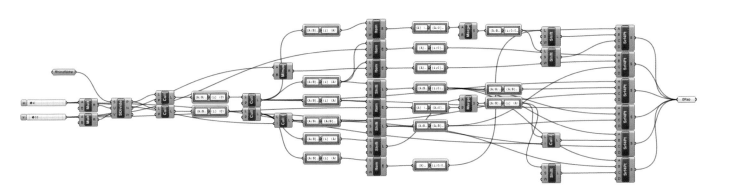

32

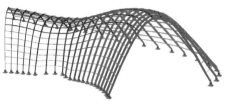

33

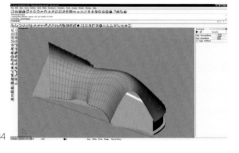

34

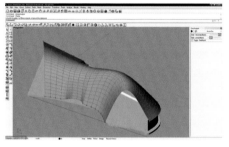

35

examples have in common is that they supplement generative design processes in terms of specialist planning analysis and as a result optimize the development process in a feedback-based way. This simulative way of working is particularly suited to geometrically complex designs, as the data chain remains uninterrupted from design stage to production and data can be extracted at any point in the process.

With each of these programming tasks there are aspects which are developed exclusively for a specific challenge, and others which could be used again for other tasks. A clearly delineated, modular structure to the programming code is important so that individual parts of code can be used for other projects and to form the foundation for office-specific digital workflows. This leads to considerable time savings when similar types of problems arise.

If you compare the previous work procedure with the classic design process – consisting of analysis, research, conception, implementation, formation of variations, and execution – you can see a shift in emphasis of the individual sub-processes (fig. 30, p. 25). The development

and formulation of concept is becoming more time-consuming and abstract – the implementation and formation of variations on the other hand take place in a directly linked-up way. Thus, when processing similar tasks, the time required for the formulation of the concept is reduced, whilst the quick implementation is retained.

There is the chance that over time, newer, quicker and more powerful planning procedures will be established through the use of programming in architecture. These procedures will not only be distinguished by integrative working with other specialist planners, but also through new design forms and concepts.

Martin Manegold, Arne Künstler

32, 33 Automatically generated static calculation model with varying grid intervals and the resulting profile strengths
34 Parametric model of the greenhouse at Trautmannsdorf castle (design: Judith Reitz, Daniel Baerlecken, BFR Lab, with Imagine Structure) in the Rhinoceros program environment
35 Competition visualization of the greenhouse at Trautmannsdorf castle
36 Schematic program structure for the interface to the calculation program

Parametric Grasshopper model Initialization of the process for a parameter	Transfer of the parameter into the Grasshopper model
Input interpretation · Define points as bearing · Segment spline curves · Calculate profile rotation · Calculate loads from surface	Output interpretation · Transfer calculated profile as Grasshopper parameter

Transfer structural data and load data

Controlling the calculation software
· Start calculation
· Evaluate results
· Save final calculation model

 If necessary alter the structural data on the basis of the evaluation and calculate again

36 Calculation software

Digital capture – terrestrial laser scanning (TLS)

There are not only digital processes as part of developing new structures – new methods of capture such as photogrammetry and TLS are used in the design of existing structures too.

In aerial photogrammetry orthogonal images are taken from an airplane and formed into image archives in a shared coordinate system. From the oriented image archive and optionally measured distance data, digital terrain models (DTM) are generated.

Close-up photogrammetry is the term for two-dimensional or three-dimensional capture of objects within a range of just a few centimetres up to 500 m. In architecture and archaeology it is used for surveying on the basis of distortion-free photographs which are overlaid with measurement data.

The equipment for capture consists of a laser measurement device, a high-resolution digital camera and a laptop. At a distance of between 1 and 2000 m from the object the most up-to-date devices are able to record up to 900,000 points per second with a minimum distance of 2 mm between points. The devices are accurate

to several millimetres over 50 m. This means images of objects such as building façades are made available which, once projected onto a surface, can be used to measure distances and lengths with the aid of a predetermined measure. In order to capture three-dimensional structures such as buildings, terrain textures or streets, reflection points are mounted at strategic positions which make processing and collating the photographs afterwards easier. Depending on the size of the building and the accuracy of the measurements, the laser in the device makes contact with the surface from at least three different viewing points and transmits these impulses to the computer. Special software combines the recorded laser impulses with the data from the camera and merges them into an integral data set. Using angles and areas of space, a trigonometric operation determines the exact coordinates of all points measured in relation to the viewing point. By transposing all images taken from the individual viewing points they are later related to the overall coordinate system of the project and turned into a 3D model. However, as only the foremost plane is scanned, this method does not

37 Grey-tone image (compressed scatter diagram) from a laser scan; kitchen at Schwarzenberg castle
38 Orthoscan (Level 1): part of the calculated longitudinal section of the south wing of Schwarzenberg castle
39 Triangular interconnection without texture: section of a room at Schwarzenberg castle

40a   b

allow the capture of any undercut or indented areas.

The major advantage of measuring with a 3D laser scanner is its speed. Compared with traditional methods of building surveying this only takes a quarter of the time and as such enables efficiency to be optimized – above all in the capture of building structures which are difficult to access such as large bridges or historical buildings. For example, one project worker can completely measure an 18,000 m² industrial plant with a laser scanner within roughly one working day. The time required to take measurements at a typical resolution is only a few minutes per viewing point. The number of scanning points, and as such the grain of the picture, determines the level of accuracy. Processing these into a 3D model takes place offsite in approximately 60 hours. Objects which are too small to be captured by the scanner can be updated using the photographic information.

A similar technique of digital data capture, though at model scale, is used by architects such as Frank Owen Gehry at the concept development phase. The planning process is comparable to that of industrial design and takes place primarily using physical models. The free-form geometries of the Gehry office cannot be adequately reproduced using conventional plans. This is why scale models are created, which a 3D measurement arm captures in three dimensions by physically reading it off. The scan provides a digital scatter diagram from which programs create a true-to-scale 3D surface model, which forms the starting point for further working steps.

This way of working leads to a continuous interaction between the physical and digital model.

The designer can use the intuitive method of model building and in parallel work with an exact digital translation of this form. The dependence on the physical

model limits the possible variations of the parametric planning technologies (see p. 24), and fact-based planning parameters are incorporated only in the following stages.

The process of capture described is also possible with stationary or hand-held laser scanning devices. This technology is often used in the preservation of monuments in order to digitally record geometrically demanding ornamentations. A laser scanner translates the original shown in fig. 40 a into geometrical data (fig. 40 b). Further processing in a 3D modelling program fills in missing segments of the geometry. Finally, a CNC mill creates a replica true to the original from a solid block of sandstone.

40   Infrared laser scan in use in the preservation of monuments
     a Original to be scanned
     b Result in the software environment

T2: Comparison of technologies available for capture

	ScannerRoland: MDX-20	Digital Photgrammetry Gom: Atos III	Infrared: 3D Creator FreeScan	RIEGL VZ-400 Laser Scanner
Method	Scanner with piezo sensor (RAPS) nearly everything scannable	Strip pattern is projected onto object/read in by 2 cameras.	Infrared and strip-light scanner with a scanning pen	Laser measurement for houses, streets etc.
Guidance	Stationary	Stationary or robots	Hand/stationary	Stationary or mobile, dynamic capture with a connection to a suitable INS system
Preparation	Not necessary	Not necessary	Not necessary	Not necessary
2D/3D capture	3D capture also for special materials	3D (measurement of undercut or indented areas with a GOM pen)	3D with infrared light diodes	3D laser
Precision (distance between measurement points)	X/Y = 0.02–0.197, Z = 0.001, in 0.002" steps	0.07–1.0 mm distance between measurement points	± 2 mm accuracy	5 mm accuracy (3 mm reproducibility)
Speed (points per second)	4–15 mm/s	Up to 4,000,000 P/s	Up to 48,000 P/s	122,000 P/s
Geometry definition	dxf, vrml, stl, 3dmf, grey grid	STL network data	STL network data	3dd, dxf, ascii, sop, 3pf, asc, tc, obj, STL, ply, pol, vrml
Software	Modela Cam, Picza	ATOS software	Geomatic, PolyWorks, Reshaper	RiSCAN PRO
Cost of device	Approx. € 4,100	Approx. € 150,000	€ 20,000–35,000	€ 84,500

Project room – the transparent project

The first building construction project whose failure is documented is the Tower of Babel: the "Babylonian confusion of languages" described in the Bible, as is well known, lead to the project being abandoned. Speaking to one another, sharing knowledge with one another – understanding one another: regulated, controlled and documented exchange of information is the basis for any form of cooperation. Communication is the most important "building material" in the planning and realization of a project.

In order to exchange information, a structured and easily intelligible connection must be set up between those involved in the project. This is only possible by using a common language, which means that communication partners must rely on the same repertoire of symbols and rules. This goes both for direct contacts between individuals as well as for their contacts within a group and naturally for contacts between groups. Everyone must be able to understand everyone else; each group must be able to communicate and be understood internally and externally.

In order to get an idea of what a virtual project room is like we have compared it in the following to "lake knowledge" as illustrated in fig. 47 (p. 31). Here all communication and all processes are represented which take place in the real world. By implication this also goes for all the supply requirements and services from any contracts which have been signed. Each piece of information is sent to and/or made available to individuals, groups or everyone according to a general rule. In this way, for example, a plan which has been entered as revision A can be followed up and can no longer

disappear from the room. If the plan is sent out to people, then this sending and receiving process is recorded in a similar way to a registered post function. As such, information flows, in accordance with the contractual agreements of the partners, and all their consequences, are visible – the project is transparent.

Virtual project room
Specialist IT providers make virtual project rooms available on the Internet. All of those directly involved in the project, such as the designers, the client, the constructors, authorities, project management and facility management (FM), form the community of project room participants. The virtual project room is configured in accordance with the project goals and organization. Access rights and working procedures are oriented on the actual contracts and are defined with the community itself. The administration of the project room and the adherence to the rules are monitored for all participants by the project management. This role can be carried out by the provider as well as by one of the parties involved in the project, e.g. the project controller or general planner with the corresponding qualifications.

Every information exchange which serves the project's goals, such as invoice and plan approvals etc., takes place via the virtual project room. Forms of data exchange are, for example, entering plans or sets of plans with a processing/coordination request or the uploading of decision templates etc. for defined participant, processing or decision-making groups. In so doing, the data follow established processing times (work flow) and distribution lists, whose defined recipients in return confirm receipt of the information within an established time

frame and must guarantee that it will be processed further.

The time behaviour of the work flow is centrally controlled in the system and compared with the time frame which was mutually defined at the start of the project. At the start it is also established at which point a time plan is deemed to be endangered, at which point an alarm should be activated, and at which point possible consequences are to be displayed. This gives those controlling the project the opportunity to take corresponding corrective measures.
As the "language" in the project room – "language" here referring to the project language in international projects but also to the agreement on formats, processes and procedures – is the same for everyone, and as such can be spoken and understood by all involved, the "virtual project room" demands and supports the systematic monitoring of and adherence to the mutually determined project goals of those involved.

Project room reproduction of models
The classic project room, in which plans as well as text and tabular data files are uploaded and made accessible for various people, has been around for over 10 years and today we cannot do without it – at least in the case of larger projects.
By gathering FM-relevant data early on in the project development and construction, it is already possible at this stage to take the logical step towards an eventual FM system with an integrated room book. This so-called RELM approach (RELM = Real Estate Lifecycle Management) is currently experiencing fundamental impulses which provide topics for intense discussion among experts at RELM conferences and specialist events.

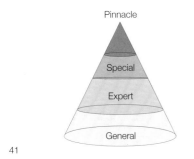

41

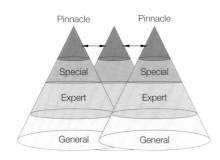

42

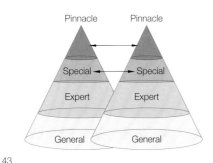

43

41 Human knowledge exchange; problem of
    communication
42 Exchange of mutual group knowledge
43 Exchange of lots of types of knowledge within
    the group

These integrated expansions reflect the original purpose of "lake knowledge" and increase its significance as a universal communicator.

Design & modelling
3D modelling, configured to the major geometries and data on the various elements, recreates each building component of a construction project in real dimensions, and on this basis is both recordable and retrievable. Modelling takes place in accordance with the specifications of the Industry Foundation Classes (IFC, see p. 34) or, in agreement with the project partners, as an original graphical data model. This project model represents the scaffold of the project and is the geometric basis for the work for all project participants. Partly interpretative reading and translating of 2D plans by the project participants is no longer necessary. Checking the overall planning process to make sure there are no conflicts is carried out in direct cooperation with all those involved in planning. After the overall planning has been completed, the traditional floor plans, sections and projections can be generated from the 3D model.

Building Information Model
Based on IFC and using computer graphics, lots of software houses develop the concept of 3D modelling further to form a building information model (BIM). This model is able to display all of the building data. Thus, it not only administers three-dimensional data, i.e. all the building component and room information including the room book, list of doors, list of windows etc., but also the fourth dimension "time". In this way building components and building behaviours can be captured and tracked throughout the duration of their usage. Particularly from the perspective of the increasing impor-

tance of sustainability and the certification processes required (e.g. LEED or DGNB certificate) these data are valuable and indispensible for the user's building management.

Obligations and laws of the project room
As the central facility for project management, the virtual project room does not only serve as a file storage system with the ability to transmit plans and documents. With the trend towards sustainable construction and the need to record all steps of the project in a comprehensible way as well as to make data needed for planning, construction and operations accessible, the virtual project room is growing in importance. Today, both nationally and internationally, it has become an indispensible element of construction projects.
Aside from the project-specific opportunities for working in the virtual project room there are also obligations which arise for project participants. Thus, everyone needs to communicate the information to be supplied by them relating to their contractual obligations via the virtual project room, and regularly retrieve data intended for them. It is not the case here, as often feared, of extra work, but of a specific rule for the project which is the same for everyone. Besides, there are definitely useful advantages to this. The permanently and seamlessly documented actions of those involved in the project within the project room are deemed to be "admissible in a court of law", which means that the point in time at which plans and directives reach recipients cannot be manipulated and above all can be referenced at any time.
Against this background, the transparent project is brought to life by all those involved in order to reach the goals set and by this to achieve the success of the project.

Highlander – "There can be only one"
Of course there are fundamental technical requirements for working successfully with virtual project rooms. A suitably powerful Internet connection, as well as the requisite software licences, are needed. The positive thing about the SaaS principle (Software as a Service) of virtual project rooms is that no hardware or software needs to be procured and as such no extra costs accrue. It is helpful to have an exact contractual agreement between those involved regarding the usage of the room and this reduces problems with acceptance right from the start. Points which need agreeing are the integration of all of those involved in the project, access rights and authorizations, naming conventions and plan keys, security and confidentiality protection and the avoidance of duplicating written documentation.

The determination and staying power of those involved in the project play an important role in the communications and work process. "There can be only one" means that in actual fact all stages of the project must be executed and documented exclusively via the virtual project room. There can be no "secondary building site" and thus no data exchange and communication without involving the virtual project room. Implementing this, the most important point for ensuring that the virtual project room, "the transparent project", works, is difficult. The human pursuit of individuality coupled with natural resistance to more control by the community can lead to individuals wanting to withdraw their participation from the project. A further obstacle can be too low a rate of data transfer which can delay the response time of the application and cost those involved their time and patience. Today, however, with low Internet costs, particularly in Germany, this is purely an infrastructure problem which is

very simple to resolve. Along with the quick reaction speed of the project room, a high level of user-friendliness is a basic requirement for its acceptance on the part of the users. This is why training sessions from user-friendly providers concentrate on explaining the agreed processes and standards displayed and not on the software. With the aim of increasing the trust of customers in the security of their data in the project room, providers are improving their security standards. Companies not only have their quality in this area monitored through their customers but also through independent institutes. Proof of test certificates e.g. TÜV, is helpful when choosing a provider. More details on this can typically be found in a technical white paper on the homepage of the provider.

If the project management (for whatever reasons) should bypass the (mutually agreed) project room in parts of the project, then it is as good as certain that a planning disaster will follow. This will probably not lead to the project being abandoned but will make the work considerably harder. If those involved then reject the use of the project room more and more as a result, there is the danger that the "communications space of the project" very quickly will become the equivalent of a hard disk memory stored on the Internet – once again. Instead of "lake knowledge" a murky data bog threatens.

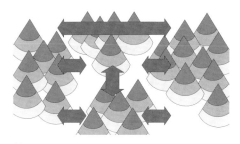

44

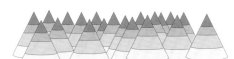

Interface medium for transferring pinnacles of knowledge

45

46

44 Exchange of group knowledge between different
    interest groups
45 Communication: connective fluidity to uncover
    pinnacles of knowledge
46 Intelligible connection of all knowledge
47 Lake knowledge – transparent project room   47

Current developments

In order to continually facilitate working with project rooms for the user these are constantly under development. One approach here is the integration of familiar communication channels, such as, for example, email, into the work of the project room. Here, several providers have managed, via a so-called email gateway, to create an option which allows those involved on the periphery, or hard-to-reach parties, to be easily included. Communication then runs via email, with all of the written documentation being recorded in the project room anyway, and, as before, all data are available in one place – a hugely important step towards increasing acceptance. Alongside this, the following minimum functions are very helpful:

- Simplicity and user-friendliness ($\rightarrow$ less training cost)
- Locating documents using full text search
- Multiple language capabilities: particularly in international projects users should be able to work in their native language
- Simple representation of procedures such as approval of plans and invoices including appropriate support in these matters
- Web-based IT support; meaning no installation cost, simple for external partners, mobile utilization

Today, virtual project rooms are indispensible both in the national and international project business. The benefits which result from their use have been proven to save time and money. It makes economic sense to use a virtual project room for projects with a construction value of approximately € 5 million or more.

Holger Heilmann

T3: Compilation of important project characteristics

Dialogue
Top3
Extrapolation on minimal requirements

Building design	Computational efficiency	GFS/(RA-C1 + RA-C 2) RA-C 1/RA-C 2	Wasted on the way areas	
			First glance optimization	
	Actual efficiency	Utilization and yield	Accommodation	Location
			Building	Complex connection
			Zoning	Infrastructure/development
			Rented areas	Orientation
			Rooms	Easy to find
			Dimensions	h × l × w
	Conceptual efficiency		Value, usage and chance of yield	
			Problems with usage	
			Problem resolutions, feasibility and cost	
	Complexity of design	Usage and demand	Necessary and formal complexity	
Construction	Constructive complexity	Efficiency and construction	Technical	Supporting structure
			Formal	Infrastructure
			Construction time	Installation
			Construction costs	Façade
			Level of standard	Light and sound
			Usage	Interior construction
Problem	Recognition Definition Resolution	Danger zones Trouble spots & Troubleshooting	**Actual** Town planning standard	**Target** Town planning standard
			Conception	Conception
			Building design	Building design
			Construction	Construction
			Building technology system	Building technology system

Digital interfaces in construction

Constrruction project organizations are characterized by the fact that the composition of project participants is heterogeneous and that the interfaces in the environment of a one-off production are highly complex. The interfaces are the result of the historically demonstrable evolution of the division of labour between the client, architect, specialist engineer, contractor, approving authorities and other stakeholders. They serve communication and the exchange of data, information, decisions and other parameters. In such complex organizational structures there is a danger of gaps appearing in the working procedures and of loss or distortion of data at the transition from one project team member to the other. It is in the interest of the construction project organization to implement and document the process chain from building design, detailed design, production planning, construction management with the help of integratively conceived, computer-supported systems. These systems coordinate the mutually dependent workflow of all participants of the planning and building process. Resulting in a coordination of the services, a documentation of the developement route and the final results.

The aim of this method to offer the client a fully comprehensible and transparent building process, in which he can steer the major decisions. This means that the client initially prescribes the system of objectives and the form that each individual element takes. Through the communication of interim results from the work of the construction project organization, a foundation is developed for the client's decisions on the continuation or modification of the path embarked upon. In this way the monetary evaluation (e.g. a cost estimation) of the status of a planning phase can lead to the client ordering certain alterations to be made to the design in order to reduce the construction costs. The key client contacts represent themselves (for example a private investor) or an organization (for example the chairman of a corporation which has awarded a building contract, as a representative of the shareholders). The rationale behind certain client decisions can be communicated to the construction project organization but does not have to be. The flows of data, decisions, finance and commodities as well as other information to be exchanged which arise in this complex time-variable project structure are part of a permanent interaction between those involved in the project – architects, specialist engineers, contractors, suppliers, authorities and the actual client organization. This interaction is regulated by interfaces defined on the basis of works and services contracts, technical and legislative guidelines (see the chapter "Legal challenges in the context of digital planning processes", p. 41ff.), the respective intended usage of information (for example, certain data sets are only generated for the internal use of a project member), as well as the tools available for data processing and documentation.

Fig. 48 (p. 34) illustrates the complexity of interfaces in a construction project organization (example with the use of a prime contractor) as well as the high amounts of information being exchanged.

The intra-organizational interfaces generally relate to the construction goal and the distribution of planning and implementation tasks connected with this within defined forms of contractor deployment on the one hand and tasks to be passed on to sub-contractors on the other hand. There are comparable interface requirements for the client, authorities, utility companies and others involved in the project, who may admittedly be external to the company carrying out the contract, but whose services are just as indispensable for the realization of the project.

It is a dynamic system based on the division of labour which is characterized by coordination and communication processes, an organization structure with qualifications and competencies, and by the utilization of resources. Its complexity increases significantly through the integration of the operation phase into the procedural structure.

The issue of interfaces in the software of the individual parties involved in the project is important for cooperation in construction project organizations.

In this context it is worth mentioning the data exchange structures of the Joint Committee for Electronics in Construction (GAEB) – a coalition of architects, engineers, public and private sector clients and the building trade, each represented by their umbrella organizations. Amongst other things the GAEB works on creating and revising standardized text for the description of building services and contract works as well as on regulations for electronic data exchange and as such provides the normative interface for the exchange of technical information in the tendering, contract award and invoicing phases between those involved in the construction (fig. 49). In addition to this the object-oriented product data model IFC (Industry Foundation Classes) should be mentioned. It is used for the exchange of

relevant data in the fields of architecture, technical building equipment and structural engineering, so that loss-free communication between the corresponding software systems is possible. The initiator of this is the international association "buildingSMART – International Alliance for Interoperability". Well-known software providers offer IFC certified software.

A systematic integration of the data and information generated in the project and object phases leads to the development of a building information model (BIM). The structure of a documentation system based on room books which, at its heart, contains a BIM visualized with fully spherical photography, is shown in fig. 50 (p. 36). It illustrates the aim when using a BIM: systematic and loss-free capture,

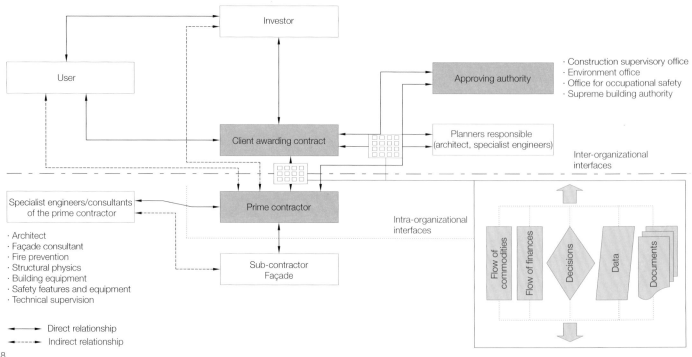

· Construction supervisory office
· Environment office
· Office for occupational safety
· Supreme building authority

Inter-organizational interfaces

Intra-organizational interfaces

· Architect
· Façade consultant
· Fire prevention
· Structural physics
· Building equipment
· Safety features and equipment
· Technical supervision

→ Direct relationship
⇢ Indirect relationship

48

preparation and long-term storage of relevant building information in a document store over the whole life cycle of a building. Of particular importance is the elimination of any losses of data still incurred at the transitions of the life cycle phases – planning – project set-up – object phase/use – caused by the working and documentation systems used. The construction industry's offensive in terms of developing software for linked-up cooperative processing and documentation of construction projects, which has already been mentioned, is coupled with the use of new working methods. In particular, a model-oriented way of working is worth mentioning, which at the very least will supplement and in many cases replace drawing-based ways of working, as has been the case in automotive, aviation and ship construction for a long time.

Computer-based model-oriented working is mirrored in automated quantity surveying, 4D simulations, animations in calculating support structures (FEM application) or in the construction of moulds for building component structures as free forms.

48 Interface definition and flow of parameters between those involved in the project
49 normative interfaces for data exchange in construction project organizations in accordance with GAEB

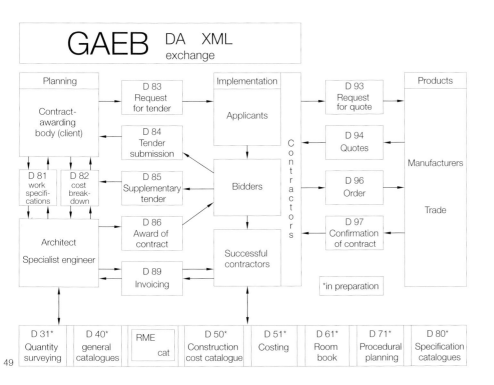

49

Model-oriented ways of working

Not just the integration of data but also the complexity of construction tasks, along with the need to couple planning, construction and operation, lead to the development of building information models (BIM). The main difference here between the usual model-oriented way of working and the drawing-oriented method is founded in their specific semantics. In drawing-oriented systems, points, lines or text trigger the interpretations of the user. In a BIM, on the other hand, the semantics is contained in the system, and as such enables complex processing by defined project workers who use the data a number of times.

With various software solutions it is possible to generate models of this type. The advantage of using software systems like this lies in the combination of CAD data and the further use for quantities as well as for generating work specifications and time schedules (fig. 52). In the 3D CAD module, elements are defined which, amongst other things, are described by quantities and qualities. The connections between the 3D objects and the quantities calculated from them are stored in the database (quantity line). From the quantity lines the items of a work specification are generated. The interconnection of these items with the stages of a time schedule enables a 4D simulation (fig. 53 a–c, p. 38).

When introducing a model-oriented way of working you need to be aware that the processes, in particular in the planning phase, but also in the construction phase, will change. For the most part, the change arises from the reuse of data and information and the interdependencies in terms of content and timescale between the sub-processes which result from this.

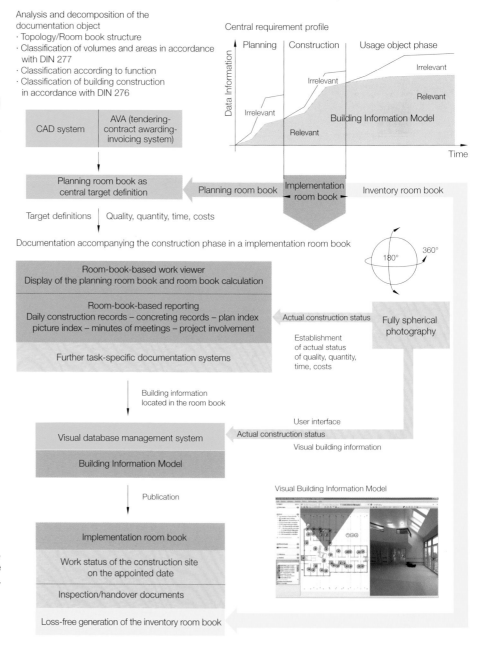

Room-book-based documentation system
The aim is cohesive capture of information at the construction phase and loss-free provision in use.

Analysis and decomposition of the documentation object
· Topology/Room book structure
· Classification of volumes and areas in accordance with DIN 277
· Classification according to function
· Classification of building construction in accordance with DIN 276

Central requirement profile

CAD system | AVA (tendering-contract awarding-invoicing system)

Planning room book as central target definition ← Planning room book ← Implementation room book → Inventory room book

Target definitions | Quality, quantity, time, costs

Documentation accompanying the construction phase in a implementation room book

Room-book-based work viewer
Display of the planning room book and room book calculation

Room-book-based reporting
Daily construction records – concreting records – plan index picture index – minutes of meetings – project involvement

Further task-specific documentation systems

Actual construction status | Fully spherical photography

Establishment of actual status of quality, quantity, time, costs

Building information located in the room book

User interface
Actual construction status
Visual building information

Visual database management system

Building Information Model

Publication

Visual Building Information Model

Implementation room book

Work status of the construction site on the appointed date

Inspection/handover documents

Loss-free generation of the inventory room book

50 Example structure of a room book based BIM documented with fully spherical photography

50 ▢ Software systems developed   ▢ Software systems used and adapted

Geo-referenced and
oriented digital photography

Interactive 4D model

Coupling process

Realistic images

Virtual images

Space

Plan and actual
status data

Time

Transformation

Transformation

Alpha-numerical data stock

Geometry and topology –
deadlines, costs, qualities, quantities

51

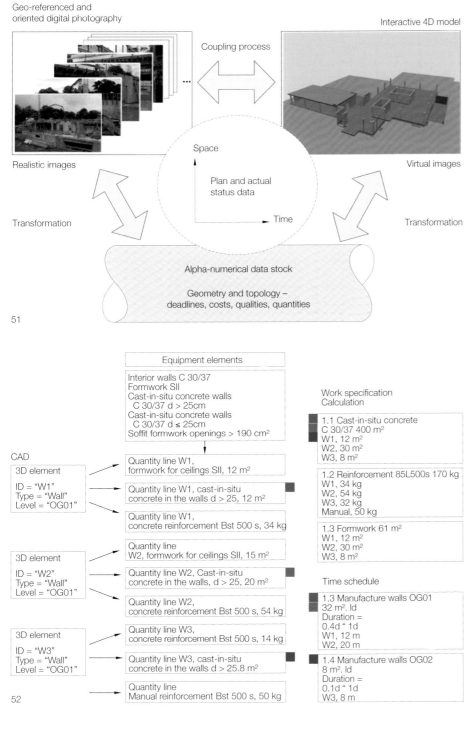

Equipment elements
Interior walls C 30/37
Formwork SII
Cast-in-situ concrete walls C 30/37 d > 25cm
Cast-in-situ concrete walls C 30/37 d ≤ 25cm
Soffit formwork openings > 190 cm²

CAD

3D element
ID = "W1"
Type = "Wall"
Level = "OG01"

Quantity line W1, formwork for ceilings SII, 12 m²

Quantity line W1, cast-in-situ concrete in the walls d > 25, 12 m²

Quantity line W1, concrete reinforcement Bst 500 s, 34 kg

3D element
ID = "W2"
Type = "Wall"
Level = "OG01"

Quantity line W2, formwork for ceilings SII, 15 m²

Quantity line W2, Cast-in-situ concrete in the walls, d > 25, 20 m²

Quantity line W2, concrete reinforcement Bst 500 s, 54 kg

3D element
ID = "W3"
Type = "Wall"
Level = "OG01"

Quantity line W3, concrete reinforcement Bst 500 s, 14 kg

Quantity line W3, cast-in-situ concrete in the walls d > 25.8 m²

Quantity line Manual reinforcement Bst 500 s, 50 kg

52

Work specification
Calculation

1.1 Cast-in-situ concrete
C 30/37 400 m²
W1, 12 m²
W2, 30 m²
W3, 8 m²

1.2 Reinforcement 85L500s 170 kg
W1, 34 kg
W2, 54 kg
W3, 32 kg
Manual, 50 kg

1.3 Formwork 61 m²
W1, 12 m²
W2, 30 m²
W3, 8 m²

Time schedule

1.3 Manufacture walls OG01
32 m². ld
Duration =
0.4d " 1d
W1, 12 m
W2, 20 m

1.4 Manufacture walls OG02
8 m². ld
Duration =
0.1d " 1d
W3, 8 m

Image information systems

Planers and contractors are obliged to report regularly to the client regarding the quantity and quality of the building services provided. The generation of these reports is currently dominated by manual processes which are supplemented by digital photography. Processes like this are not very effective because the effort required to archive and search for data to reconstruct a certain status during the construction phase takes up valuable time.

The model-oriented way of working can be extended by further digital processes. In the following, the explorative prototype of an image information system is introduced, which, faced with 4D models, has extended functionalities and processes these integratively. The system was developed at the Institute for Construction Operations at the Technical University in Darmstadt. [1] Throughout the whole construction process, the system connects a digital building model with digital images and in this way documents the construction progress and the quality of the construction (fig. 56, p. 39). The starting point of the system called "BIS Bau" is an object-oriented 3D model of the building to be constructed, which contains all elements as parameterized objects (amongst other things, construction elements of the building shell, elements of the technical building equipment or the façade). The structure of the building model is adapted to the building processes and the model is digitally accessible to all project participants. By connecting geometric data with further attributes such as material qualities, structural-physical variables, surface finish, costs and deadlines, a 4D model is generated.

51 Conception of an image information system used by a BIM
52 Model-based processing of a construction project – multiple usage of the basic data

53   a–c Screenshots from the software iTWO, which
          document the model-based way of working –
          integration of all processes in an object core
          including 4D simulation

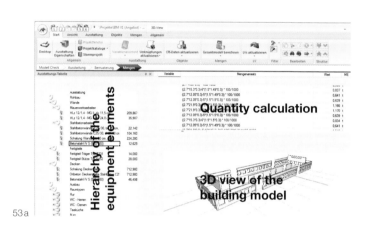

53 a

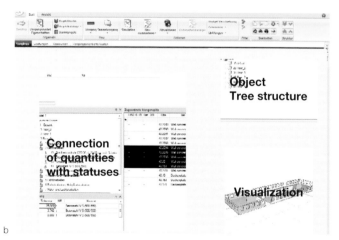

b

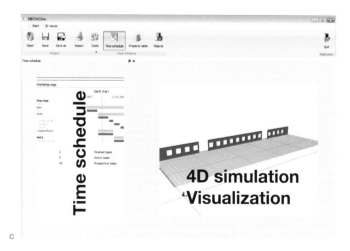

c

The core functionality of BIS Bau includes the integration of actual data, in particular of geo-referenced and oriented digital photographs of the real object. For this purpose, a sensor-controlled positioning system was developed, which is shown schematically in fig. 55. Its distinctive feature is that the system enables the positioning and orientation of images and the identification of construction elements contained within these in interior spaces. An example of its application in the field of documenting works and quality is shown in the series of pictures in fig. 56a–d. Several geo-referenced and oriented digital photographs, together with the 4D model, document the status of the building. In fig. 54, standpoint and viewing direction of the picture sections captured by the camera are displayed as segments of a circle. This documentation of the standpoint is automatically generated by the recording system in the computer. In the sub-frames, the semi-automated (as it is always supplemented by verification by an operator) process of status identification of construction progress is displayed between the real picture and the section of 4D model. The expert operator, however, will always have to check that the information generated by the computer conforms to reality. This makes it clear that the computer systems discussed cannot replace the specialists/experts, but rather support their work. The prepared building model contains all the elements of the contractually defined work statement (plan data) such as plans, descriptions of services or any technical contract requirements relating to the construction parts to be built. In this way, a comparison of the contractual building target of a construction element with the construction work completed in reality and documented using the system is possible at any time.

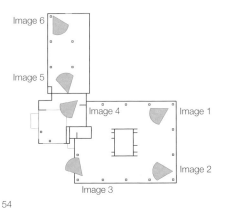

Image 6
Image 5
Image 4
Image 1
Image 2
Image 3

54

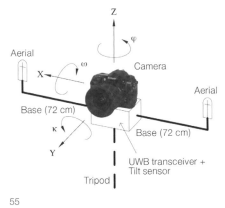

Z
φ
Aerial
X
ω
Camera
Aerial
Base (72 cm)
Base (72 cm)
κ
Y
UWB transceiver +
Tilt sensor
Tripod

55

Furthermore, the realistic depictions of the digital photographs, in connection with the space-time structures of the 4D model, capture the implementation of works in accordance with the contract in a believable and verifiable form. All building processes or individual actual building statuses can be reconstructed without risking misinterpretations, as details of the floor, room, time and construction part, as well as further information such as the contractor doing the work, technologies used and any faults discovered during construction, are all available. It is also possible to verify beyond doubt if preparatory works or works which are later concealed have been carried out. Measurements of building components can be checked with the aid of image measurement in the 4D model. To determine the location of objects, digital images are taken from one standpoint at two different heights or from different standpoints and transferred into a corresponding evaluation system. Using the photos, as well as measurements, it is also possible to check surface qualities (e.g. porosity of concrete surfaces or paint structure).

The image information system also provides the possibility of developing inventory documentation which provides all the verification needed for clients or other project stakeholders such as authorities or utility companies. The system is also helpful in achieving certifications, for example, the LEED certificate. In addition, the client can develop visualized digital user handbooks for tenants or for administration purposes on the basis of the documentation. Using a system like this, the user can, for example, call up the building as a geometric structure and then access within this the relevant information on a particular building part by simply clicking on it, without having to look through confusing lists.

The image information system, which was developed as an explorative prototype, was tested in the realization of the "inHaus2" building project in Duisburg in 2007/2008. The results confirm the validity of the approach chosen, which is being researched further.

Sensors
The developments in the field of digital processes are inseparably connected to the development of sensors. One example to mention is interactions in virtual environments as they are increasingly seen in architecture in the case of bidirectional reconciliation or checking of planning statuses or tracking alterations (design review). The interaction in immersive virtual environments, in which reality and simulation merge for the operator, is not created with the help of keyboard and mouse, but with the help of sensors which continuously calculate the position and orientation of the observer and thus enable interaction with the objects of the virtual environment. [2] The development of intelligent sensors, which support the geo-referencing of digital photographs in a digital building model, was also necessary for the image processing system shown before. Developments in the field of process engineering, augmented by the monitoring of logistical chains or material flows, are only possible as incredibly rapid developments are currently taking place in the field of sensors. In the following, two sensor technologies are compared: radio frequency identification (RFID), which has already found its way into construction, as well as NanoLOC technology [3], which is currently at the developmental stage.

RFID is a radio technology for automatic identification by means of which digital data, which are found on so-called tags, can be written and read off using a hand-

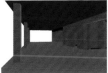

56a

b

c

d

54 Allocation of the viewing points
55 Schematic measurement set-up for indoor positioning
56 Picture series – geo-referenced and oriented digital photographs of the real object (left) and the corresponding sections of the building model (right)
   a Section of image 1 in the model
   b Section of image 2 in the model
   c Section of image 3 in the model
   d Section of image 4 in the model

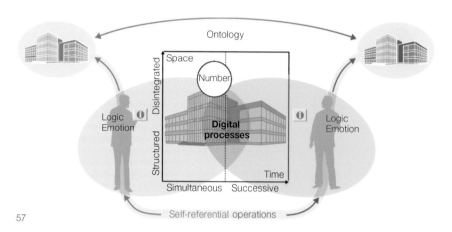

57

held device. The tags are attached to building parts or objects and generally contain information on just these objects. RFID technology is used in various sectors, amongst others in aircraft construction, in wholesale, in the moulding industry or in healthcare. RFID tags are mainly used as:

- Barcode substitute: attaching a label (Electronic Product Code) which can be read automatically provides the possibility of monitoring the whole logistics chain from production through to the consumer.
- Protection against theft

Further possibilities for application are controlling access, approving machines, the documentation of work processes, mobile time capture, positioning and locating as well as managing rental property.

Although the advantages of RFID technology have been recognized in many fields, the technology is still at a developmental stage. This has to do, amongst other things, with the following problem areas:

- High costs of some components such as the reading device
- Susceptibility to water getting into it, static discharge or high magnetic fields (e.g. lightning strike)
- Unauthorized persons could destroy RFID tags irreversibly and without touching them (vandalism)
- Shadowing: it can happen that even nearby tags find themselves in areas with no reception
- Reach: RFID tags cannot be read well if conductive obstacles are present between the tag and reading device.

One possible solution to these problems is NanoLOC radio technology. The core of this technology is the NanoLOC chip, which, based on Chirp Spread Technol-

ogy (CSS) enables both data communication as well as distance calculation with the aid of Chirp impulses. This high-frequency radio module works on the 2.4 GHz ISM band which is freely available worldwide. The chip has a standardized interface and as such can independently gather the data described in the following. Through the high bandwidth of the impulses (80 MHz) NanoLOC systems boast the following features:

- 3D positioning of objects: each NanoLOC radio hub is able to determine the spatial distance to any other hub, both indoors and outdoors. Through the possibility of networking, a positioning system for dynamic networks with movable hubs can be set up. The anticipated positional accuracy is 2 to 5 m indoors. As such, for example, the location of ready-made concrete parts in a room can be determined, both at the construction stage and in the finished building.
- Immunity against shadowing due to the diversity of frequencies available
- Security: as a result of the CSS procedure and additional encryption, NanoLOC systems are immune to all attempts at tapping into them by unauthorized persons.
- Reach of up to 900 m in the open and 60 m in buildings – can be extended as desired through the option of networking
- Reliable connection even under bad conditions
- Sensor technology and data transfer: the NanoLOC transceivers provide the opportunity to control further sensors and to relay the data received. A fully equipped computer is integrated into the NanoLOC transceiver, which enables data to be received, modified and relayed.
- Electricity consumption: due to the low level of energy consumption and the compactness of the NanoLOC mod-

ules, NanoLOC technology appears to be suited for setting up an energy saving sensor network. In addition there is the option of operating the NanoLOC systems as zero energy systems under certain conditions.

The digital processes shown in the previous sections are the foundation for BIM systems and are conducive to a model-oriented way of working. A 4D visualization accompanying the project, and the creation of building information models, along with real time detection using sensor systems, open up the possibility of transparent status descriptions of all project and object phases.

Christoph Motzko

57 Digital processes as the central element of communication in construction project organizations.

Legal challenges in the context of digital planning processes

Increased digitalization leads to a compression and dynamization of various procedures in the context of the design and construction process. Through this, on the one hand, potential for increases in effectiveness and quality arise. On the other hand, the architect is confronted with new technological, organizational and administrative challenges. From a legal standpoint questions such as the following arise:

- As regards collaborative projects with division of labour, who is responsible for what?
- Are modern means of communication such as email and virtual data rooms suited to verifiable information and documentation purposes?
- Within which terms and by which deadlines do planners have to fulfill their obligations?
- What possibilities does remuneration legislation offer in terms of securing an adequate remuneration in light of the increased technological demands made on planning?

Responsibilities in collaborations
The architect has the main role amongst all those involved in design and construction. Correspondingly this comes with a strict level of liability. From the particularly trusted position which the architect holds in relation to his client arise, above all, increased obligations to advise and make suggestions. Working together with division of labour between the architect, specialist experts and building contractors, however, leads to overlapping circles of responsibility and as such often to combinations of mutual liability. In the case of an error in monitoring construction on the part of the architect, both architect and building contractor are liable jointly and severally to the client. The client can choose from whom he claims back the total damages. A subsequent attempt by the architect or the architect's liability insurance company to seek recourse from the building contractor for a claim which has been filed against the architect or the insurance company often fails because the building contractor is insolvent. The number of company insolvencies rose to nearly 34,000 in 2009 – a further increase is expected for 2010.

In the case of architects and specialist engineers working together, inherently each is solely responsible for their area of work; by its very nature there is no joint liability. It is different, however, if:

- The specialist engineer makes inappropriate factual assumptions – which are recognizable to the architect
- The architect does not detect errors in an engineering process in the case of details which are part of the general knowledge of an architect (e.g. the requirement of slip and expansion joints – Superior Court of Justice, ruling of 13.12.2005 – 6 U 140/01)
- The architect does not recognize contradictions in an engineering process (e.g. different reinforcement strengths in the reinforcement plans compared to those in the main structural analysis – Higher Regional Court Schleswig, ruling of 11.04.2006 – 3 U 78/03)

In each case, above all, careful coordination and intensive monitoring is needed on the part of the architects. It is they that are responsible for ensuring that all specialist contributions interlock as they are supposed to; they should not accept the work of third parties without criticism.

A particular obligation to exercise due care arises from the so-called trustee position of the architect: this means that architects are the first contact and most important representative of the client throughout the whole planning and construction activity. In this sense they must assist the client in enforcing his requirements of the other parties involved in construction and design (e.g. claims for compensation for faults and damages). In general they must also inform their contractual partners of their own mistakes (most recently, German Federal Court of Justice, ruling of 23.07.2009 – VII ZR 134/08).

This particular position of trust with the resulting trustee obligations distinguishes the architect from specialist engineers and building contractors. Digitalized planning processes with a multitude of – seemingly coequal – stakeholders, however, run the risk that architects are not able to fulfil their role as trustee. However, exactly this leads to a stricter level of liability than with other parties involved in the planning process. In order to do justice to the demands resulting from this situation, above all in the context of advising the client, architects must actively fulfil their central role in the design and construction process with the necessary assertiveness. In doing so they should constantly be aware that they can also be liable for the work of others involved in the project (e.g. project managers, specialist engineers).

Email and virtual data rooms
Modern planning processes are inconceivable nowadays without the application of electronic means of communication such as email and the use of data rooms. However, electronic communication is not equally suited to all the reports that need to be made to the client

or third parties in the course of a project. In the case of the question of whether an electronic declaration is just as valid as a written one, i.e. a declaration set down on paper, in German law, the principle of freedom of form applies. A declaration is fully valid regardless of whether it is submitted in writing, verbally or through conclusive behavior (e.g. a hand movement or gesture) or else by email. However, there are exceptions. For certain declarations the written form is stipulated, for example, for the building application (§ 60 no. 5 of the Hessian building code) or for agreements regarding remuneration where the intention is to deviate from the minimum rate (§7 paragraph 6 HOAI, Fee Structure for Architects and Engineers). In the case of contracts according to VOB/B (German construction contract procedures), for example, the written form is stipulated for giving notice of cancellation of (§§ 8 no. 5, 9 no. 2 clause 1 VOB/B) as well as for formal acceptance (§ 12 no. 4 clause 2 VOB/B).

If this is the case then it is not possible to invoke the intended legal consequences with an email.

If the written form is not stipulated then declarations made by email are also valid as soon as they are delivered to the recipient of the declaration. The deciding factor here is the point in time at which, under normal circumstances, the recipient has the possibility of taking note of the declaration. This prerequisite is fulfilled when the email is accessibly saved in the mailbox of the recipients or their provider. If this happens after close of business then the declaration is only considered to be delivered on the next working day.

If emails contain an eligible electronic signature in accordance with the Signature Act, then, as a general rule, they are deemed equivalent to a document in the written form, as here verification of iden-

tity is possible. This distinguishes them from "basic" emails where the sender cannot be definitely identified. Eligible electronic signatures use a private key saved on a Smart card which is scanned into the PC after a PIN is entered into a supplementary device. Architecture software systems are already available which have integrated signature components.

In order to be able to verify, in the case of a dispute, that the email was actually delivered to the recipient, the sender must prove delivery to the recipient. It is being discussed in legal circles, but has not yet been clarified, if proof is made easier for the senders if they have a confirmation of receipt from the recipient, as in this case too manipulation cannot be ruled out. The same applies in questions of access and verifying access in the use of Internet-based data rooms.

Due to the uncertainties connected with checking access, email and data rooms must currently remain means of communication limited to the exchange of information. In the case of declarations relevant to contractual or liability law, a verifiable delivery form is to be preferred.

Terms and deadlines
The dynamism of digital planning processes also has a significant effect on the provision of services of the architect in terms of timing. Modern means of communication create the expectation that information is always available immediately everywhere. In contrast with this, intellectual processes, such as the development of an architect's design, as before, need time regardless of all the digital support. This is why discrepancies can occur between the expectation of the client and the ability of the architect to provide services. This implies a high risk potential for architects, as their profes-

sional indemnity insurance does not cover damages for delayed provision of services.

The question is at which point in time the architects have to deliver their service. Here we need to differentiate between the terms deliverability, due date of the service and default in the provision of service.
- Deliverability: the point in time after which it is possible for the architects to provide their service. In this case architects should make sure they set their client terms for approval or that corresponding terms are agreed in the contract.
- Due date: the point in time after which the client can demand the service from the architect
- Default: from the start of a default the client has further claims on the architect available to them (e.g. compensation for default) right up to the possibility of cancelling the contract.

If no deadlines for the architect's services have been agreed by the contractual partners, then the due date is based on the consideration how much time is appropriate for the service in accordance with the circumstances of the individual case (Higher Regional Court Düsseldorf, ruling of 29.11.1996 – 22 U 116/96). However, for both sides, what is considered "appropriate" may be in dispute.

If the contractual partners have agreed deadlines for the architect's services, then the architect's services are due in line with the contractual agreement. This does give a higher degree of calculability but at the same time increases the time pressure for the architect.

If the architect fails to deliver despite the service being due this does not automatically imply that the architect is in default. Here, as a rule, a reminder is required, which must be issued after the due date.

Important exceptions: a default due to delay without a reminder occurs as soon as the due date has arrived if a calendar deadline was set (for example: "completion of construction design draft: 30.11.2009"). The same is true if the due date is linked to a clearly defined occurrence and the deadline for this occurrence can be calculated in calendar terms (for example: "approval of the implementation and assembly design of the building contractor within 6 working days upon receipt by the architect"). Consequently, in the case of determining a calendar date or being able to determine when the architect culpably exceeds the deadline, this can lead to the occurrence of default and thus to claims by the client for compensation which are not covered by the architect's indemnity insurance.

As a consequence, the architect should take the following precautionary steps to avoid exceeding due dates and defaulting:
• Permanent, office-internal checking of terms and deadlines
• Documentation of the reasons for delay if caused by others involved or the client themselves (in so far as the architects are not to blame, § 286 paragraph 4 BGB (German civil code)
• Immediate notice to the client of the circumstances which are causing an obstruction (if possible in written form with verification of delivery).

Due to the lack of insurance protection the architects must focus their attention particularly on providing their services on time. If others involved, or the clients themselves, cause delays, then the architect must always give notice of this to the client immediately. If, for example, a neighbour, who comes from the "sphere" – the area of responsibility – of the client, stops the start of construction, then whilst the clients are not the direct cause of the delay, it is nevertheless attributed to them (so called sphere theory).

Remuneration law
Technological advances require investments and cause ongoing costs. The remuneration law provides possibilities to compensate additional costs through a higher remuneration. The service descriptions – and as such also the binding remuneration of the HOAI – only incorporate such services as are generally needed to carry out a task in accordance with the regulations. Remuneration for other services can be freely agreed separately (§ 3 paragraph 2 and 3 HOAI, 2009 version). If costs are incurred by the architect through additional IT expenses, the question is raised of whether these are services which are generally needed to carry out the task in accordance with the regulations. If this is not the case, then contractual partners can freely agree additional remuneration.

Even if modern tools such as CAD and virtual data rooms are standard in current practice, they are not yet included in the service descriptions – e.g. for buildings and extensions forming rooms in accordance with appendix 11 to the HOAI. This allows for the assumption that, according to the way the legislators see things, instruments of this kind are not needed to carry out a task in accordance with the regulations. For the architect, this constitutes an argument for a possible separate and free remuneration.
The catalog of special services in appendix 2 of the HOAI is a further argument in favour of this (e.g. figure 2.6.2 buildings and extensions forming rooms). According to this, the "production of depictions through various techniques, such as, for example, perspectives, templates, models" represent a special service in the context of the preliminary planning. Digitally generated 3D models, which are admittedly normal today, albeit not generally required for carrying out a task in accordance with the regulations, can also fall into this category. Therefore, a separate and free remuneration is also possible for this.
In addition there is a new ruling on additional costs in § 14 paragraph 2 no. 1 HOAI: here, costs for transferring data are specifically mentioned. According to this, fees payable to the Internet provider can be invoiced as additional costs alongside the main remuneration fee, either verified on an individual basis or – in the case of a written agreement at the award of contract – as a flat rate (§ 14 paragraph 3 HOAI).

The HOAI provides basic approaches to generating additional remuneration by means of contractual agreements. For each service that goes beyond that which is deemed to be generally needed to carry out a task in accordance with the regulations, the contractual partners can agree separate remuneration alongside the HOAI basic remuneration. However, to do this the architect needs a solid knowledge of remuneration law.

Axel Wirth

Notes:
[1] Pflug, Christoph: an image information system to support building process controlling, diss., Institute for Building Operations, TU Darmstadt, 2008
[2] Encarnaçao, José Luís: Cyber-technologies as tools in construction. In: IT changes building. Building Foundation, Stuttgart 2008
[3] Mehr, Oliver; Norrdine, Abdelmoumen: RFID and NanoLOC compared, report, Institute for Building Operation, TU Darmstadt, 2009

Digital production technologies

Around 98% of the planning, calculation, optimization, tendering and marketing in construction is based on digital data. Along with this comes a more and more direct interface between the computerized design process and the physical implementation. This chapter explains production technologies which allow seamless digital control. It provides knowledge and competencies which contribute to the strategic selection of production techniques. This will stimulate you to look at innovative architectural concepts and eases communication with engineers, specialists and contractors.

Digital production technologies are divided into four principal areas:
· Generative procedures – also called primary shaping – describe technologies whereby a component part is manufactured from formless material, e.g. tiny particles. Transferred to the architectural setting, larger construction elements are made from small individual parts (e.g. 3D printing).
· Subtractive procedures sever the cohesion of the component part at the point where it is processed. Here differentiations are made between cleaving, machining and removal procedures (e.g. milling).
· Transformative procedures retain the cohesion of the material and generate component parts through a lasting alteration to the shape of the unfinished parts. Generally this allows for the optimization of their initial condition (e.g. bending).
· Joining procedures increase the cohesion by the long-term connection of several component parts (e.g. welding). This procedure is not elaborated upon because the level of automation in the architectural field is not yet developed far enough.

The chapter focuses on rule-based, modifiable procedures which allow for finely gradated numerical control of the process steps. The overarching logic of rule-based planning (see chapter "Digital planning technologies", p. 24) supplies the information and data base for the procedures illustrated. The production technologies described enable design information to be transferred to production without an interface.

Computer-based methods lead to an increased efficiency in design. Thereby even a smaller architect's office can give itself competitive advantages over large competitors. To achieve this goal and to implement sophisticated architecture convincingly, an understanding of the production technologies is a basic requirement.
Examples which have been executed or are at the prototype stage illustrate each of the procedures. Transferring them into a realized project makes it possible to grasp the potential of each technology.

1   Numerically controlled robot making plastically formed openings in a wall, Gramazio & Kohler, ETH Zurich

Generative procedures

2

The term "generative" is derived from the Latin word "generare" – generate, produce.

Chemical and physical processes create solid bodies with the material qualities of the basic product from formless materials such as fluids, powders, gases, fibres or chips. As the material is being specifically formed for the first time these procedures have a great deal of flexibility and high economic potential. Among the most important primary shaping procedures are manual casting and blow moulding as well as numerically (by data) controlled sintering, expansion and extrusion.

In the 1980s, stereo-lithography was developed to a level suitable for use in the market as the first generative procedure. By now there are around 50 different generative procedures with different physical and functional principles. They can all be used during a product development chain from the idea generation phase through to production and make it possible to manufacture component parts with unrestrictedly complex geometry and individually formed surfaces – even in a small quantity. However, restrictions in the choice of material have to be accepted. For the production, three-dimensional geometric data from a CAD model, which serves as a foundation, are divided into individual planes, which build up the desired form layer by layer. There is particular potential in the manufacturing of multi-material construction parts, whereby primary shaping procedures are combined with follow-on procedures. The demand on the speed of the procedure is indeed growing constantly, but the main development potential lies in the further development of suitable raw materials.

Rapid procedures

Various generative procedures come under the overall term "rapid procedures". The well-known "rapid prototyping" (RP) is the collective term for generative procedures which produce preliminary stages of end products. The aim is to manufacture a physical 3D component part quickly and without using manual procedures on the basis of CAD data. In doing this, complex geometries are reduced to a large number of overlaid 2D production steps.

Meanwhile, amongst the rapid procedures, clear areas of application and concepts have established themselves, to which belong terms such as rapid prototyping for building prototypes or rapid manufacturing for direct end production. In addition, terms such as concept modelling for the construction of concept models and rapid tooling for the construction of tools define the areas of application of these procedures even more precisely.

The most common format for rapid procedures, which most 3D modelling programs also provide, is the STL format. Via this abstraction of the data interface, the project is subsequently transferred to the production procedure.

There are three generative methods which follow the principles of construction in layers and enable the scaling of construction projects:
- Construction with precast concrete components: CNC controlled construction with pre-cast concrete components is limited to two-dimensional construction parts such as walls, which, however, can be manufactured in a highly integrated way.
- Robotic layering procedures: a computer breaks down the geometry of construction elements such as, for exam-

ple, clay bricks or timber construction elements, into the form of large pixels. The layering in differentiated construction forms is carried out by a multi-axis gripper robot.
- Rapid manufacturing at a scale of 1:1: so-called contour crafting and the D-shape procedure transfer the principle of rapid procedures to the production of models or prototypes at a scale of 1:1 for construction. The methods work with a material similar to concrete which builds up the geometries of construction parts layer by layer.

Table T1 shows the most significant technologies and the state of the art as a comparative overview. The procedures described above are particulary suited for application in construction. Most of the procedures are still at the prototype stage for architecture; however, this can be expected to develop quickly induced by the complexity of new construction forms.

In architecture, rapid procedures are used primarily for the quick and cost-efficient production of highly complex, individual and durable models, templates, prototypes and construction elements up to a maximum size of 1 × 1 × 1 m. They are ideally suited to "mass customization" i.e. customer-specific mass production (see p. 50) and production on demand.

2   Translation of a complex spatial sketch into a data set using 3D software and into a physical model using a 3D printer.

46

T1: Overview of the most important generative procedures with a comparison of the most important process parameters for the designer

Technology	CNC precast concrete parts	Multi-jet modelling (MJM)	3D Printing (3DP)	Fused Deposition Modelling (FDM)	Selective Laser Sintering (SLS)	Stereo-lithography (STL)	Contour Crafting (CC) D shape	Robot-based layering
Construction material	Polymers Thermoplastics Acrylonitrile butadiene styrene (ABS) Wax	Polymers Thermoplastics Acrylonitrile butadiene styrene (ABS) Wax	Silicone Ceramics Aluminum Plastics Cement Concrete	Polymers Acrylonitrile butadiene styrene (ABS) Wax	Polymers Polyamides Polycarbonates Polystyrene plastic-covered sand	Polymers Epoxy resin Vinyl ether resin Acrylic resin	Artificial sandstone	Bricks Wood
Maximum construction size (mm)	10,000 3,000 500	298 185 203	600 500 400	600 500 600	720 500 450	1000 800 500	6,000 3,000 3,000	3,000 3,000 3,000
Precision	± 5 mm	± 0.5 mm	± 0.2 mm	± 0.2 mm	From ± 0.1 mm to ± 0.02 mm	± 0.05 mm	± 20 mm	± 10 mm
Options for finishing processes	Glazing Polishing	Sandblasting Polishing	Infiltration Sintering	Heat treatment Epoxy resin or painting Grinding	Infiltration with epoxy resin or metals which melt down	Sandblasting Grinding	Plastering Grinding Insulating	Plastering Grinding
Geometry data input	.dxf .dwg	.stl .iges .step	.stl .iges .step	.stl .iges .step	.stl .iges .step	.stl .iges .step	.stl .iges .step	.stl .iges .step
Manufacturer	3D Systems	3D Systems	3D Systems	Stratasys	3D Systems	3D Systems	Monolite UK	KUKA Prototype-Development ETH ZÜRICH
Time/mm Construction height/m^2	10 s	45 s	20 s	90 s	120 s	150 s	60 s	10 s
Application	Construction industry	Automotive industry Porcelain industry Design	Model construction Design industry Architecture	Model construction	Electronics industry Office machines Automotive industry	Model construction Electronics industry Medical technology Jewellery industry	Construction industry Large prototypes	Construction industry

3

The automotive industry and medical technicians use this procedure, for example, to manufacture finished components. The speed of manufacturing allows component parts to be checked at an early stage, not only in terms of their geometric form and aesthetics but also their functionality. This serves the rapid improvement of the product or design.

Further benefits are:
- The data set can be altered at any time and as often as required.
- The material supports itself; no support structure is needed.
- Expensive tools are superfluous.
- A high level of complexity is possible.
- Precision (accuracy of 0.25%)
- Further processing e.g. painting is possible.
- Cost-effectiveness

As a result it is not the quantity but the material and time required for the work which determine the price.

Rapid procedures are above all of interest when they can replace costly precursory processes such as milling or mould construction, or when a large number of slightly differing construction parts need to be made. In this way, for example, a complex joint hub can be sintered directly from the final material such as metal, which is a very cost-effective method and economical in terms of material. In the following, five rapid procedures are introduced in detail which can be usefully applied in construction for model building.

Stereolithography – STL
Inside the equipment is a fluid, light-sensitive synthetic material. The laser travels over this raw material and hardens it at specific points. After each step the component drops several millimeters lower into the fluid. The end products are compounds similar to plastic with very delicate construction dimensions. For example, a machine like this can manufacture objects up to 300 × 300 × 500 mm in size. The stereolithography procedure is particularly suited for architects as a method for building models. In a short space of time they can examine complex geometries using physical spatial models. The procedure generates 10 mm of geometric volume in approximately 8 minutes.

Selective Laser Sintering (SLS)
In a basin there is a powder which is pre-heated to just below its melting temperature. A data-controlled laser travels over the basin corresponding to the predefined contour. The powder absorbs the energy of the laser at specific points, which leads to locally restricted sintering or melting of the particles. Sinking the platform by 1–3 mm determines the resolution of the geometry. After the platform has been layered with a further coat of powder the cycle begins again, and a further layer is built up. Fine polyamide (which may be reinforced with glass or carbon fibre), elastomers and ceramic powders are used as materials. Using SLS, actual usable products, such as the foldable stool ONE_SHOT.MGX, (fig. 7), can be produced in a continuous process. The seat, legs as well as all the movable joints are created in one procedure. The chair is sintered in its closed condition from white polyamide and can subsequently be unfolded in a fluid motion. The product has a slightly porous surface typical of the procedure due to the powdered form of the material.

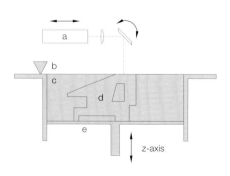

4

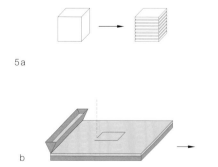

5a

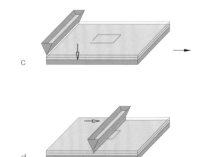

6

7

Selective Laser Melting – SLM

Metal Laser Melting came onto the market in 2002. Comparable to the SLS procedure, a metal powder is melted specifically using a laser beam and bonded to the layer beneath it. With this technology, tools, moulds and individual components as well as medical implants in 100% solid steel, cobalt chrome, gold and titanium can be produced. The procedure enables the manufacturing of construction parts which are put under a lot of strain such as joints which vary from one another in a supporting structure. When manufacturing a lot of self-similar construction parts this procedure is economically superior to production with individual casting moulds.

Three-dimensional printing – 3DP

In this procedure powdered construction material is distributed in a defined way by computer-controlled printer jets and stuck together in layers using a binding agent. The construction part is manufactured on a platform which is lowered by the depth of one layer at a time. As the construction material is self-supporting, no supporting material is necessary. Three-dimensional printing has limits in terms of the stability of the construction parts created, how-

ever, in contrast to the other procedures described, it allows components to be realized in dimensions up to 1 × 1 × 1 m.

Fused Deposition Modelling – FDM

FDM is also a layering procedure. A heated extrusion jet applies a thermoplastic synthetic material along the geometry of the construction part on a construction platform, which is lowered after each layer. The hot material from the extrusion jet binds with the already pre-set structure below it. As the construction material hardens slowly, a supporting material is needed for the construction process. This has a lower melting point to the construction material and is melted off after the printing has finished.

In all RP disciplines people are currently trying to reduce the comparatively high costs in order to appeal to a broader spectrum of users. For rapid manufacturing, research is being carried out into thermoplastic synthetic materials which are more stable and can be applied with smaller tolerances.

In the service sector, laser sintering is currently slightly quicker and cheaper than FDM and 3DP and is being used for serial production at the end of the design

chain. FDM has the advantage that the cost of supervision and space needed are less than with laser sintering, as no post-curing facility is required. The machine costs are cheaper with FDM compared with laser sintering. Material qualities in FDM are continually being improved and are nearing those of laser sintering.

3   Laser-sintered model, Centre Pompidou Metz (F) 2010; Shigeru Ban, Jean de Gastines
4   Construction principle of a stereolithography machine with a liquid bath and laser deflection
    a Laser
    b Slide
    c Liquid bath
    d Construction object
    e Work platform
5   Process cycle of a stereolithography procedure
    a Geometry divided into horizontal 2D cross-sections from 0.1–0.2 mm in height
    b Exposure of the powder using a computer-controlled laser beam
    c Lowering of the platform by the height of a layer of powder
    d Loading with new powder
       Thickness of layer: approx. 0.1 mm
6   Lamp whose parametrically scalable "leaves" are produced by means of a rapid manufacturing process.
7   Foldable stool, ONE_SHOT.MGX (h = 650 mm, Ø = 110 mm (folded), h = 400 mm, Ø = 320 mm (unfolded)) by Patrick Jouin
8   Bag with movable stitching; rapid processes allow the construction of dynamic structures.
9   Bag, zoomed in on the movable structure of the stitching

8

9

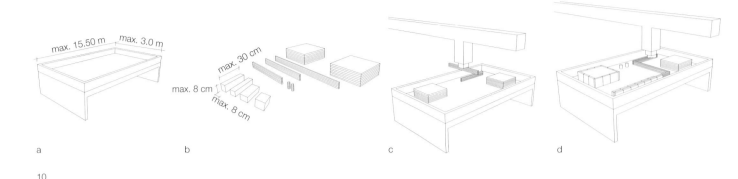

max. 15.50 m   max. 3.0 m

max. 30 cm

max. 8 cm

max. 8 cm

a

b

c

d

10

CNC precast concrete elements

Traditional precast concrete elements are moulded by hand; this is why special shapes, openings and inserts can only be made with a large degree of manual effort. This process, in the procedure described here, is carried out by a CNC-controlled moulding robot. Framing elements are positioned on horizontal moulding benches using CAD data and are fixed with magnets. The robot inserts the prefabricated concrete reinforcement and fills predefined areas with concrete. Individually segmented walls can be produced quickly and economically. The level of efficiency with computer-aided production can be a factor of 3.7 times higher than with manually produced prefabricated components. With this method, some 50 production pallets can be produced in 8 hours – that is the equivalent of approx. 110 walls.

Due to the moulding benches and the place holders the procedure is limited to two dimensions. The maximum size of the construction part is subject to the limit for usual transport sizes (12 × 3 × 0.5 m), primarily in terms of the height of the construction part. The potential of the method lies in the possibility of producing parametric structures efficiently. This is how the idea of "mass customization" finds its way into solid construction. Fine variations can also be realized in system building construction without additional costs. Furthermore, the robot-controlled procedure allows the construction parts to be prefabricated in a highly integrated way. It is possible to link additional functionalities, such as insulation layers, building equipment and appliances or specific structural requirements, into the production process. This means that the cost of assembly on the construction site can be significantly reduced. Building in additional items, such as windows or interior construction layers, can increase the degree of prefabrication still more.

Future potential for development lies in the possibility of moulding and producing variously curved construction parts, being able to do without inserting concrete reinforcement thanks to new fibre-reinforced and load-adapted concrete mixes, and by this means further optimizing production.

Robot-aided assembly of individual elements

The D-Fab research group at the ETH Zurich has been researching the development of additive procedures on a construction scale since 2003. One of the classic techniques in the construction industry is the layering of brickwork. Since the early 1980s there have been numerous attempts to automate this process, which, however, could not be successfully implemented due to the sensitivity of the machines used. The driving force behind the research of the ETH is not only the desire for increased efficiency but also for higher performance and a new aesthetic appearance of the building material.

The research project uses a 6-axis industrial robot which prefabricates brick walls.

A thin-layer adhesive joins the layers of bricks and absorbs thrusting pressure during the transport of the prefabricated construction elements. In order to develop the design of the walls a 3D modelling software is used. The transfer of this to the construction robots takes place using an individually developed program. In a prototype construction

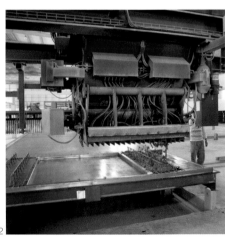

11

12

 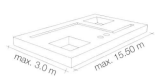 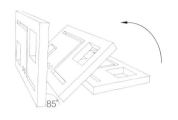 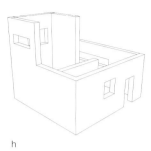

e f g h

project a wall of approx. 200 m length was created for the Swiss Biennale pavilion in Venice (fig. 14). The possible advantage of the robotic production of brickwork compared to manual work is the capability of the robot to position each brick differently without the extra effort of measuring and moulding. In order to take advantage of this the architect must have software which defines the spatial configuration of the brick wall.

Two routes are taken in order to check the positioning of the bricks. In the first method the spatial configuration is projected onto the wall and each brick is rotated around its central axis; from this, logarithmic patterns are generated. The second method is based on a more intuitive approach: the architect generates and shapes surfaces under the consideration of specific structural parameters, such as minimum overlapping of bricks and maximum overhang, using 3D modelling software. Then, a program projects bricks onto the geometry of these surfaces. The design data are directly used in order to generate the control data for the robot. Additional programming work is not required – an economically relevant factor, as frequently the design cost

increases disproportionately with the number of individual elements. Fabrication is carried out with the help of a commercially available jointed-arm robot with a range of $3 \times 3 \times 8$ m, which can lift 110 kg. An epoxy resin is used as mortar, which reaches far higher levels of strength than traditional mortar. This means that additional reinforcement between the layers of bricks, which could only be expensively integrated into the building process, is superfluous. The production unit, shown in fig. 13, needs approx. 30 seconds to lay a brick and costs €150,000 in its standard configuration.

The procedure was used in the realization of the 400 m² façade of the Gantenbein winery in the Grisons. The façade protects the interior space from direct solar radiation. It consists of 72 segments which were transported to the construction site in prefabricated form. The price of the prefabricated brick elements, which could only be produced by hand at considerable expense, is approx. €110/m². The future ideal is a fabrication robot which can carry out the assembly directly on the construction site.

10 Sequence of production of CNC precast concrete elements
   a Horizontal steel benches with steel contour moulding
   b Variable steel frame elements
   c CNC-controlled positioning
   d Fixing with magnets
   e Introduction of concrete and compaction by shaking the bench
   f Setting time approx. 6 hours, removal from the moulding
   g Vertical positioning using pivoting bench
   h Transport and assembly
11 Preparation of the moulding bench with robot-controlled positioning of moulding elements
12 Automated introduction of concrete controlled by the programming
13 D-Fab robot in the production process with a moving unit which increases the working space
14 Robotically produced brick wall at the Biennale in Venice (I) 2008, Gramazio & Kohler

 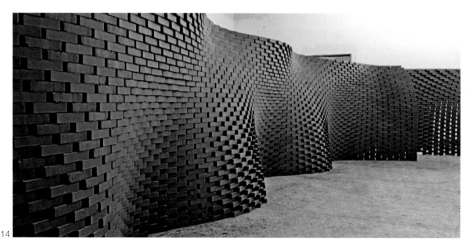

13   14

Size of system	7.5 × 7.5 m
Height	3 / 6 / 9 / 12 / 18 m
Max. print size	6 × 6 m
Number of jets	300 at 20 mm between axes
Jet action time	10–15 ms
Control unit	PC-PLC Siemens with Profibus
Power supply	380 V – 220 V – 50 Hz
Grain size metrics	0.1–60 mm
Productivity	30 cm with two rotations
Operating personnel	2
Pixel dimension	5 mm
Min. layer thickness	5 mm ± 0.5 mm
Max. layer thickness	60 mm
Weight (excl. refill mechanism)	1300 kg
Weight (incl. refill mechanism)	5000 kg

15

3D printing on a large scale

For construction, the scaling of manufactured products is of interest. In England (D-Shape) and the USA (Contour Crafting), research is being carried out into 3D printing procedures which enable the production of constructions/construction elements up to 6000 × 6000 × 6000 mm; this could be the future of free-form construction without moulds.

The D-Shape procedure, developed by engineer Enrico Dini, transfers the principles of 3D printing to construction in a scale of 1:1. It is based on 2–10 mm thick layers of sandstone particles, which are bonded by an inorganic binding agent.

The design process corresponds to the usual 3D design process. The geometric data of a design are checked structurally using Finite Element Software, optimized if necessary and then translated into STL data. This data set is then transferred to the computer which controls the D-Shape print head. Then the production process begins which is comparable to the printing process of a classic inkjet printer. The system alternately distributes sandstone particles and binding agent to defined points. The production process takes place as a continuous cycle which produces all construction elements immediately without an auxiliary structure. The construction grows upwards in 5–10 mm steps; each layer is able to support the following one. The curing time of the whole structure requires approx. 24 hours.

Currently the technology is at an advanced prototype stage as there is still considerable potential for improvements in efficiency and speed. The machine is made up of a 6 × 7.5 × 7.5 m aluminium framework which defines the con-struction space. The structure is very light; therefore, it is easy to transport and can be set up in just a few hours. With the current technology, buildings or construction elements up to a surface area of 6 × 6 m can be produced without manual intervention. The height of the construction is, in theory, unrestricted and primarily limited by the ability of the construction material to support its own weight. At the corners of the construction, electro-pneumatic compactors raise the apparatus up with a degree of accuracy of 0.1 mm. On the horizontal plane a computer guides a print head with 300 jets along a bridge and deposits particles in accordance with the CNC-defined path. The feed rate varies between 0 and 500 mm/s.

The most important innovation of the procedure lies in the development of a suitable material system for large-format 3D printing. The D-Shape procedure uses a "structural ink", a chemically refined sandstone dust with low viscosity and high surface tension which has an unusually high interlacing capability. This makes a fast pulsing rate possible for the jets. It is a two-component system which is made up of a solid material and a fluid inorganic binding agent. The solid material is distributed in layers by a slider, whilst a low-maintenance jet adds the fluid component. This binding agent is distributed amongst the granular material and, thanks to its extremely fine grain size, forms a homogenous mass. The granular material, for example sandstone, has a range of granularity from 0.01 and 65 mm and is actively involved in the catalytic reaction. It is a mineral

15   D-Shape configuration in a large-scale test and
     machine parameters of the D-Shape system

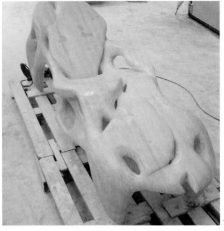

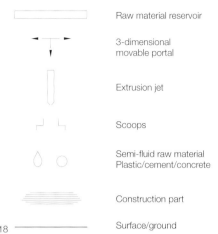

16   17   18

Raw material reservoir

3-dimensional
movable portal

Extrusion jet

Scoops

Semi-fluid raw material
Plastic/cement/concrete

Construction part

Surface/ground

material which, thanks to its microcrystalline structure, has a high hardness grade and high tensile strength. The catalytic reaction happens very quickly so that the compound cures in a short space of time and develops a tensile strength which is close to its final tensile strength. Fibre reinforcement (glass fibre, carbon fibre or nylon fibre) can be added to the process. This increases the tensile strength and the rigidity of the material system. The process transposes sand, powder or gravel into its original stone form; the artificial stone that results is very similar to marble.

The radiolarian structure serves as a prototype reference object. The three-metre-high monolithic sandstone structure was produced in two weeks; the material used costs approx. €70 for sand and binding agent (fig. 19 and 20).

Contour Crafting – CC
In the USA, work is being carried out on a comparable procedure – Contour Crafting. The extrusion procedure was developed by Behrokh Khoshnevis at the University of Southern California in Los Angeles. Research is also being carried out there into specific raw materials for the

procedure, such as quick-setting concrete. The Contour Crafter uses digital geometry definition which, as in the D-Shape procedure, is divided up into horizontal layers. In production the CC needs a constant influx of semi-fluid construction materials such as plastic, cement or concrete, which cure quickly, so that it can cope with the pressure of its own weight from subsequent layers. The computer-controlled spray jet of the Contour Crafter distributes thin traces of the construction material on the surface, which are then given their final form by two scoops fixed at the side. In order to erect structurally stable walls the CC robot can construct hollow walls to begin with, which, as a second step, it then fills with concrete; a lost casing, so to speak, is created.

The vision of the large-scale 3D printing procedure is to produce demanding geometries without expensive moulding structures directly on site, and this within a day without using manual labour. There is even more potential for improvement with this procedure. The prognosis for the future suggests that this will depend on the use of inorganic, ecological and cheap binding agents.

16   D-Shape production process where the first printing layer has been applied to the work bench
17   End of the production process after the application of 400 layers in a working time of 18 hours
18   Layering principle of the D-Shape procedure
19   3D model of the structure
20   Finished structure, which is free of left-over particles

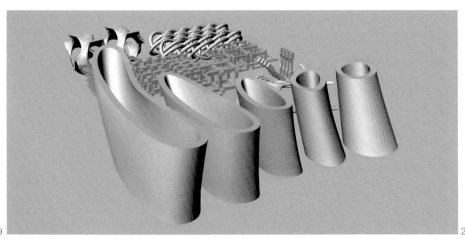

19   20

Subtractive procedures

Procedures which separate materials, or subtractive procedures, serve the local dissolution of a material's cohesion. Here, particles are separated from the raw material so that the final volume of the construction part is reduced.

In the most important procedures a distinction is made between cutting and machining processes. Particular attention is on procedures which can be controlled by CNC data and therefore enable a direct interface between digital design and implementation.

Cutting is used to separate flat raw material shapes where the thickness of the material varies little. A distinction is made between shearing, jet cutting and thermocutting. In the case of shearing, also known as nibbling, a die head is guided over the component part controlled by CAM. The consistent die head carries out an up and down movement at numerically determined positions, which separates the material (sheet metal up to maximum 10 mm thick). Shearing is a purely 2D procedure, as the shearing head's dimensions would be a hindrance in 3D processing.

In the case of jet cutting, in contrast to conventional shearing, no cutting edge is used for separating material parts, but rather a jet. This is either made up of bundled energy (laser jet cutting) or a medium such as gas (torch cutting, plasma cutting) or water (water jet cutting). Therefore, jet cutting techniques display a high degree of flexibility in relation to the materials to be cut and cutting conditions. One benefit is the very low level of material loss along the edge of cut. This allows friction-locked connections to be achieved through a direct, perfectly fitting cut. A jet cutting head guided by a robot arm can also process

three-dimensional construction components, for example, tubes.

Plasma or gas cutting uses an electrically conductive argon gas thermally heated up to a high temperature. A jet focuses the gas to a high energy density and guides the plasma at a speed of more than 350 km/h in the direction of the component part. The plasma arc achieves temperatures of up to 30,000 °C, which, in connection with the high kinetic energy, can generate a very high cutting speed depending on the thickness of the material. It is imperative that the component parts are electrically conductive.

In the case of processing with machining, generally called milling, a motor sets the tool in a rotating motion and then guides it over the component part. Milling machines are only suitable as purely two-dimensional blank cutting tools. 3-axial, 5-axial and 7-axial machines, however, provide the option of producing component parts with highly complex geometries. This leads to a flexibility of application both for processing sheets as well as solid materials. The machines can be equipped with milling heads of varying sizes which have a corresponding machining volume depending on use. The type of milling head also determines the range of material that can be processed. The technology is primarily used in processing wood and plastic materials. However, mineral and metallic raw materials can also be processed using high-grade milling heads.

Large-scale hot-wire cutting is the most exotic of all the subtractive procedures, which is very well suited to concrete formwork and the manufacturing of light, voluminous construction parts. In this procedure comprehensive CNC control is used. The hot wire remains linear, however,

through a continuously adaptable guidance position and a rotatable component part, high-quality, specific geometries can be manufactured. Expanded materials such as polystyrene or styrodur are used.

Overall, subtractive procedures provide a lot of potential for realizing individualized construction forms in architecture. In choosing the method, however, the question of material economy continually arises. For example, it does not appear sensible to mill a specific individual component from a block of solid material if there is not decisive added value in doing so.

Table T2 gives a comparative overview of the most important technologies with the parameters which are decisive for the construction industry and the state of the art.

T2: Overview of the most important subtractive procedures with a comparison of the most important process parameters relevant for the designer Before commissioning, a comparison of the cost-effectiveness and any necessary finishing is recommended. The manufacturing of processing templates may be worthwhile.

	CNC punch TruPunch 5000	Lasering	Water jet (pure)	Water jet (abrasive)	Nibbling TruMatic 5000	Plasma cutting MicroStep	Milling 2-axial Bima 310	Milling 5-axial HERMLE C50U dynamic	Robotic lasering (multi-axial) ABB IRB 6650S
Material	Sheets of steel, stainless steel, brass, aluminium and copper	Almost all materials	Rubber, plastic, foil, textiles, plywood, foam, paper, foodstuffs	Concrete, harder metals, glass, ceramics: also multilayered and combination materials	Sheets of steel, stainless steel, brass, aluminium and copper	Conductive metal, raw materials	Wood, (aluminium), foam, cardboard	All common types of material including soft plastics	All common materials
Material thickness	Up to 8 mm	400 mm (tube diameter)	Up to 350 mm	Up to 350 mm	Up to 8 mm	3000 mm	Up to approx. 250 mm (with 100 mm drill)	Ø 700 mm to Ø 1150 mm	Dependent on laser
Size of construction part	2550 × 1280 mm 3070 × 1660 mm	4000 × 3000 mm 6000 × 2000 mm 16 × 2.5m	3000 × 4500 mm	2000 × 1000 mm 4000 × 3000 mm	2500 × 1250 mm 3000 × 1650 mm	30,000 × 8000 mm	1450 × 3900 mm 1630 × 5000 mm	Ø 700 mm to Ø 1150 mm Large-scale mill up to 15 × 60 m	Almost any, Arm: 3.9 m
Speed (depending on material)	1400 strokes/min	300 m/min	35 m/min	35 m/min	1200–2800 strokes/min	6 m/min	Approx. 10 m/min	Up to 40 m/min	Dependent on laser
Accuracy	± 0.1 mm	0.05 mm	0.025 mm	0.025 mm	0.03–0.01 mm	0.2–0.5 mm/ depends on type of material/shape	0.1–0.2 mm	Very accurate, in the µ region	Dependent on laser
Quality of cut	$^2/_3$ of the length is waste edge	Very good, may leave behind black marks	Rough to very good	Rough to very good	$^2/_3$ of the length is waste edge	Not a consistently smooth cut surface/ surface roughness	Ribbed to smooth	Very good	Dependent on laser
Waste caused by tool	0 to 3 mm	0.1–0.5 mm	0.1–0.25 mm	1 mm	0 to 5 mm	0.8–1.5 mm	1 mm, dependent on the milling head	Slight, dependent on tool in to the µ region	Dependent on laser
Finishing needed	Yes, grinding the edges	Dependent on the material	Dependent on the material	Dependent on the material	Yes, grinding the edges	Yes, grinding	Grinding	Not necessary	Dependent on laser
Possible to parameterize	no	yes	yes	yes	no	yes	yes	yes	yes
Geometry options	2D	2D (3D)	2D	2D	2D	2D (3D)	2D (3D)	5-axial 3D	Multi-axial (6) 3D
Overall energy consumption	25–50 kW	100 kW	37 kW dependent on pump	37 kW dependent on pump	25–50 kW	Approx. 80 A	18 kW	39–60 kW	Dependent on laser
Control data	e.g. dxf	e.g. dxf	2D construction data, e.g. dxf	2D construction data, e.g. dxf	e.g. dxf	e.g. dxf	dxf, dwg, IGES, STEP	IGES, SEP	Dependent on laser
Interim software	TrueTops	TrueTops Laser	No, plug & play	No, plug & play	ToPs 300	AsperWin	Imawop	e.g. ITNC 530	Mechanical cut/dependent on laser

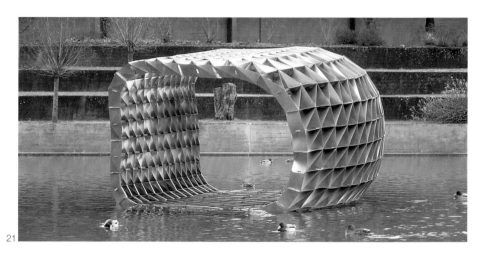

21

CNC laser cutting

Cutting with a high energetic light beam (laser) is one of the thermal separation procedures. The beam is generated in a laser medium through the influx of energy and then tapped off in a controlled way. The raw material being cut absorbs the energy contained in the laser and, as a result, heats up intensely in a very short space of time. Then a process gas blows the melted material from the incision downwards.

The procedure was first used as a cutting method in the 1970s. Since the middle of the 1980s autonomous laser assemblies and cutting systems have been being built whose power and cutting speed continue to increase.

Laser cutting is suitable for construction parts whose cut forms (fig. 22) are complicated or whose forms vary within a series. In combination with CNC-guided machine programming new possibilities for the development of construction parts open up. Forms which have been designed, simulated and calculated on the computer can be turned into real constructions quickly and efficiently. Free forms can be easily realized as, in the case of CNC laser cutting, the ability

to modularize and the reproducibility of individual elements does not play a role. The processing size for component parts is limited by the size of the machine; large-format portal lasers (up to 10 × 50 m) are already in use in ship building. For industrial processing carbon lasers and neodymium lasers (ND:YAG) are used. By way of example, a machine with a power of 6000 W is able to cut – within a working range of 6 × 2 m – construction steel (up to 25 mm), aluminium (up to 15 mm), stainless steel (up to 20 mm), zinc (up to 20 mm) and copper sheet (up to 20 mm). The device is controlled along an x and y axis and evens out any inconsistencies in the sheet with an automatic z axis adjustment. The laser described is a CO_2 melting cutter. The advantage over blow-torch cutting (using additional oxygen) is that the metal is not oxidized and hence smooth cutting edges, which are not discoloured, are produced. By introducing oxygen during burning, significantly higher temperatures arise. As a result of this, on the other hand, the blow-torch cutter is superior to the melting cutter in economical terms, because it manages to cut sheets of the same thickness using significantly less energy.

Today the maximum processing speed is approx. 40m/min, which allows a high level of economic efficiency to be reached. If the laser is configured perfectly then the cutting edges (fig. 23) do not need any follow-up processing. The procedure is virtually abrasion-free and, although the energy consumption is relatively high, it is comparable with mechanical processing methods for identical construction parts. By specially guiding the laser head it is also possible to process tubes (fig. 24). When doing this the laser beam needs to be the same distance from the component part permanently.

CNC model-building laser
Laser technology is well suited to architectural model building. Dxf or dwg data define the paths of the laser beam using

21 SXM pavilion, ETH Zurich (CH) 2001, consisting of 974 differing elements made of stainless steel sheets with a thickness of 1.5 mm; the construction parts were cut and achieve the necessary inherent rigidity through the angle of bending.
22 Laser-cut large-scale construction parts show that the technology does not have any restrictions.
23 Cut edge quality; in most cases finishing is not needed.
24 Special laser robots enable 3D construction parts such as pipes to be cut.

22

23

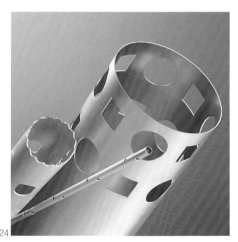

24

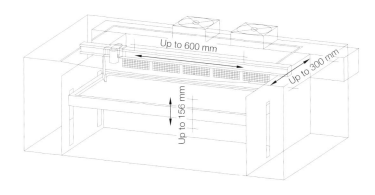

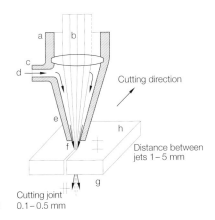

25

26

T3: Comparative table of model construction materials; natural materials are best suited for processing with a laser

	Thickness	Speed/min	Revolu-tions	Suitability	Cutting/engraving
Brown cardboard	1.0 mm	3.8 m/min	1	+	yes/yes
	1.5 mm	1.5 m/min	1	+	yes/yes
Finnish cardboard	0.5 mm	6.0 m/min	1	+	yes/yes
	3.0 mm	1.2 m/min	1	+	yes/yes
Grey cardboard	0.6 mm	4.2 m/min	1	+	yes/yes
	3.0 mm	1.5 m/min	2	+	yes/yes
Black cardboard	1.0 mm	2.3 m/min	1	+	yes/yes
Basswood	1.0 mm	3.0 m/min	1	+	yes/yes
	6.0 mm	2.0 m/min	3	+	yes/yes
Solid wood Lightweight plywood	0.5 mm	2.5 m/min	1	+	yes/yes
	2.0 mm	1.7 m/min	2	+	yes/yes
MDF/HDF	1.0 mm	2.0 m/min	1	+	yes/yes
	6.0 mm	1.0 m/min	3	+	yes/yes
Formica (good to process) Plastics Polystyrene	0.3 mm	5.5 m/min	1	+	yes/yes
	2.0 mm	4.0 m/min	4	+	yes/yes
Plexiglass	0.5 mm	5.0 m/min	1	+	yes/yes
	8.0 mm	1.0 m/min	5	+	no/no
Glass				–	no/yes
Fabric				+	yes/yes

vectors, similar to an inkjet printer. 2D drawings are used for producing model construction elements out of two-dimensional materials. Production runs along the same lines as with large-format laser blank cutting. During processing the component part is either fixed to the lifting table by a vacuum or is held in position by small magnets. The laser can either cut or engrave the material and in doing so can process nearly all solid-state materials. The engraving can serve as coding or positioning markings for assembly later on.

If the dimensions and material thickness of the model are true to the scale of the original then the system can be structurally checked. The designer can evaluate both the overall system and the individual construction elements in detail. The exchange between computer and model optimizes the construction principle step by step. Due to the accuracy of production it is possible to join the model construction elements together with compartmentalized plug-in connections. CNC-guided model building is an efficient way of supporting the design process which is now frequently transferred completely to a virtual space with physical objects.

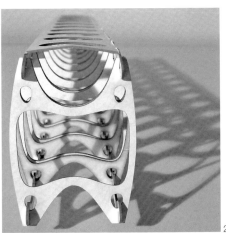

27

28

25 Professional laser with working space dimension of 1000 × 6000 mm
26 Composition of a laser cutting head
    a Cutting jet
    b Laser beam (bundled light)
    c Lens
    d Process gas
    e Focused laser beam
    f Cutting beam
    g Cutting material which has been blown out
    h Component part
27 Organic bridge cross-section out of cardboard, the manual production of which could only be carried out at high cost
28 Model construction laser in the production of repetitive elements

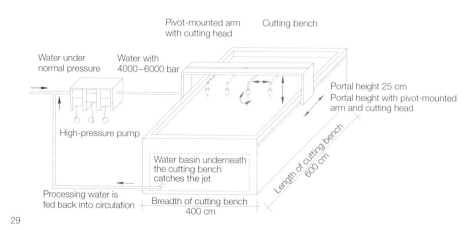

Pivot-mounted arm
with cutting head

Cutting bench

Water under
normal pressure

Water with
4000–6000 bar

Portal height 25 cm
Portal height with pivot-mounted
arm and cutting head

High-pressure pump

Length of cutting bench
600 cm

Water basin underneath
the cutting bench
catches the jet

Processing water is
fed back into circulation

Breadth of cutting bench
400 cm

29

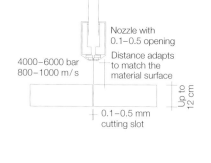

Pure water cutting

Nozzle with
0.1–0.5 opening

4000–6000 bar
800–1000 m/s

Distance adapts
to match the
material surface

Up to
12 cm

0.1–0.5 mm
cutting slot

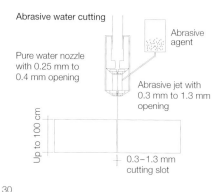

Abrasive water cutting

Abrasive
agent

Pure water nozzle
with 0.25 mm to
0.4 mm opening

Abrasive jet with
0.3 mm to 1.3 mm
opening

Up to 100 cm

0.3–1.3 mm
cutting slot

30

31

CNC jet cutting

In architecture, CNC jet cutting is used primarily for 2D blank cutting of solid materials such as stone, metal or plastic. It is fully CNC-guided on the basis of vector data and enables the production of complex geometries with fine contours. In this procedure water is formed into a jet which comes out of a cutting jet at up to 1000 m/s. In doing so the potential energy is turned into kinetic energy which gives the jet its cutting effect. Whereas pure water cutting for processing mainly soft materials (e.g. paper, plywood, insulating materials, foams, plastics and textiles) uses just the jet energy of the water, with the abrasive procedure there are also additional grinding particles in the cutting jet. The abrasive agent (e.g. garnet sand) is introduced to the mixing chamber via a small opening in the cutting head where it is mixed with the water jet. A downstream abrasive nozzle focuses the mixture which is then emitted with a diameter of 0.5–1 mm. In this way it is also possible to process hard materials which are very thick, such

as stainless steel (up to 400 mm), copper, titanium, glass, stone, concrete (up to 180 mm) and ceramics. Multi-layered materials can also be cut without problem. The processing time increases exponentially with the thickness of the material.

The technology even enables the cutting of irregular surfaces as, unlike laser cutting, no specific point of focus in the material is necessary. The cut edges of the water jet cutting technology require as good as no finishing. A machine of this type (fig. 29), for example, has a working surface of 4 × 6 m, upon which material thicknesses of up to 500 mm can be cut.

Due to the quick computer-controlled configuration of the machines, custom cutting even of a small number of units or one-off productions is cost-neutral. As the procedure is not limited to particular materials, material thicknesses or forms it is used in nearly all branches of industry.

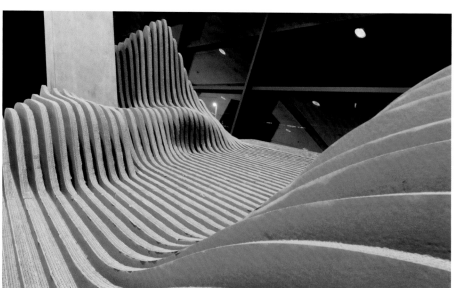

32

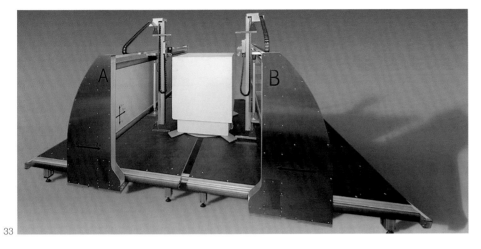

33

Technical data

Max. block size	5100 × 1350 mm
Working area	5000 × 1250 mm
Block depth	Up to 5000 mm
Max. positioning speed	3000 mm/min
Cutting speed	50–1000 mm/min
Positioning accuracy	< 0.1 mm/300 mm
Repeat accuracy	0.05 mm
Contour accuracy	± 0.2 mm/m
Power supply	230 V/50 Hz – 1500 W
Computer control	Standard PC

CNC hot wire cutting

This technique gives the architect the possibility of efficiently producing large-volume geometries. The spectrum ranges from independent construction elements, such as components for three-dimensional sandwich elements, to form parts as a basis for further production steps. In this procedure a heated CNC-controlled wire processes a foam material. Even with the largest current computer-controlled 4-axial hot wire cutting systems, which cut objects from expanded or extruded polystyrene foam, CNC processing guarantees absolute precision and reproducibility. The volume weight of the raw material can be between 15 kg/m³ and 50 kg/m³. The technique is used in the production of oversized forms such as ships' hulls or the blades of wind turbines. The mechanical construction of the machine consists of two portals made of aluminium system profiles and a guidance and driving system mounted on a chassis. The distance between the portals and the length of the cutting wire stretched between them are variable and adapt optimally to the parts being manufactured in order to produce accurate results. The raw material blocks are manoeuvred into the machine from the front using roller conveyors, which makes it possible to handle even large and heavy blocks without a problem. The x axes are set out as roll guides on 10 mm steel shafts. A multiphase motor with speed reduction gears moves both axes along this construction with the help of gear racks and thus guides the heated cutting wire through the component part. In the case of conical cutting contours an electronic wire tension device balances out the change in length of the hot wire. The cutting software regulates the temperature of the cutting wire via a transformer and controls the whole system. The control PC is located in an independent control box together with all of the electronics. The machine can be optionally equipped with two vertical cutting wires for vertical processing of form parts. By travelling over a component part multiple times, highly complicated geometries are viable. Once finished, the foam elements are initially delicate. In the next step a GRP coating, on a layering or spray basis, is applied in layers to protect the construction parts; this means that they are also suited for use outdoors. Large volumes are produced from combined construction elements whose butt joints are glued and covered over with cloth and putty.

With CNC hot wire cutting objects with finely varying gradations can be produced in a cost-effective way. The technology is well suited for temporary constructions as well as for creating prototypes on a 1:1 scale.

34

29 Composition of a jet cutting machine with a work bench of 4000 × 6000 mm; large portal machines can reach dimensions of up to 10 × 20 m
30 Comparison of pure water and abrasive water cutting
31 Varying cut qualities of steel; by reducing the speed of the procedure the quality of the cut increases.
32 Exhibition stand of the TU Darmstadt at HOBIT 2008 made from 84 varying cut segments of corrugated cardboard; it was produced using a continuous CAD-CAM jet-cutting procedure; the cutting jet is so quick that the cardboard does not get soaked through during processing.
33 Machine with technical data which represent the construction space
34 Bus stop in Hoofddorp (NL) 2003, NIO Architecten; the structure is manufactured from polystyrene foam and measures 50 × 10 × 5 m; the surface is protected by a layer of GRP coating. The construction costs were €1 million; in concrete or steel they would have been twice this.

35

CNC milling

Milling refers to the processing of metals, wood or plastics by machining with a milling tool. In architecture the potential of this method lies primarily in multi-axial processing of hard construction materials. Two-dimensional objects can be milled simply from sheet goods. The milling data are generated by the designer using standard CAD programs. The milling program controls the milling depths and the speeds of operation. It makes sense to simulate the milling process before work begins in order to identify any potential programming errors. Two-dimensional CNC milling is used for materials which can only be processed with difficulty with laser or water jet. In this instance the milling head acts as a blank cutting tool. Disadvantages of the procedure are slow processing speed, high level of material waste caused by the milling head, and the restriction to milling-head-specific radii at internal corners.

For three-dimensional objects, a 3D file, mostly in STL format, is used. Nearly all modern 3D CAD systems generate this file format and provide simple exchange of data. The milling program sets the tool parameters, the feed rate of the machine, and the accuracy, and displays this information as an NC program. Up to 7-axial

machines can be programmed via a CNC control system. Varying milling heads are selected from a changeover store depending on the requirements in terms of surface finish, precision, or speed. In order to generate complex 3D contours the milling tool travels across the component part along many parallel paths. With multi-axial mills the component part can be processed at unrestricted angles, which enables the production of sophisticated 3D contours. However, it is worth noting that undercuts are difficult for the machines to realize; rotating the component part or the tool are the basic possibilities for producing construction parts which are processed from all sides. The exact positioning of the component part on the milling bench in relation to the system zero point is fundamental for the precision of the processing.

5-axial milling is used in timber construction, steel construction and mould construction. In timber construction, for example, continually changing glued laminated girders are processed using the mill. Multi-axially processed wood-based material or hard foam serve as the negative form for thermal forming of glass or plastic. The amount of material used, however, is high, and therefore economically and ecologi-

36

T4: Comparison of types of robots

	Max. range [mm]	Effector bearing load [kg]	Repeat accuracy [mm]
Small-scale robotics	350–850	2.5–10	< ± 0.025–0.05
Low bearing loads	1503–1911	6–16	< ± 0.01
Medium bearing loads	1991–2429	30–60	< ± 0.15–0.2
High bearing loads	2600–3500	100–240	< ± 0.2–0.25
Heavy loads	2826–3326	360–570	< ± 0.15

37   38   39

cally questionable. In metal processing 5-axial mills are used for manufacturing specific joint hubs, which can replace the use of the cast metal process for smaller series.

CNC milling is admittedly the most variable of the subtractive procedures, however, a comparison with alternative production procedures should always be carried out in order to find the most economic solution.

Jointed-arm robotics

Robotics enables a considerable increase in the efficiency of complex construction processes. The most important components of robots are the control system, manipulator and effector. A motor moves the links of the kinetic chain. Robots are not limited to one function. According to requirements they change automatically from effector A (laser cutting) to effector B (laser welding). Industrial robots vary in their range, the load they can bear, and their repeat accuracy (see table T4). The repeat accuracy describes the precision with which the robot produces multiple component parts or the degree of variation between them.

The jointed-arm robot in fig. 39 is extremely flexible over 6 axes; its radius of action is up to three metres. We distinguish between three basic principles in

the programming of robots. In the case of process programming, the human calculates the working steps exactly in advance and enters them directly as information into the program system. In the case of teaching, the robot is manually taught how to proceed by a human guiding it through various working steps. The control computer records the movements and actions. This method is used today for complex tasks. In the case of self-teaching the robot uses a camera or sensors to capture where objects are located and decides itself how to act. This method is the most sophisticated and requires the robot to have programmed intelligence.

For construction, jointed-arm robots are of particular interest, as they can operate as universal, programmable processing machines. A 7-axial jointed-arm robot is generally a 6-axial robot with a linear travelling unit, which increases the working space. Alternatively the component part is moved within the working space of the robot. The guidance of the linear unit is integrated into the robot control system as a mathematically coupled axis. Since as high a level of prefabrication as possible is becoming more and more important in construction, there is a lot of potential for industrial robots in taking over complex subtasks. As in machine building

they can be used for carrying out repetitive but slightly varying working processes. These include constructing façades, preparing timber construction parts, and the reconstruction of natural stone façades in the preservation of monuments. On the construction site, however, the use of robots is only worthwhile in a limited way, as their mechanics and electronics are too delicate and the precision suffers.

35   Driftwood pavilion which was created using a 3-axial mill from large-scale wooden planks, AA-London (GB) 2009
36   Working space of a fixed-position jointed-arm robot, approx. 3000 × 3000 × 3000 mm
37   Tool changer which automatically changes between different milling heads
38   Digital simulation of milling paths; this method helps to avoid mistakes when working on a valuable component part.
39   Jointed-arm robot with a rotational axis, two joints, and a rotating actuator head
40   Large-scale mill: 4-axial milling process on a real component part which is producing a topography model
    a   5-axial milling
       Working space   Accuracy
       x axis: 60 m   x axis: ± 0.8 mm
       y axis: 12.5 m   y axis: ± 0.5 mm
       z axis: 7.0 m   z axis: ± 0.3 mm
    b   The component part can be layered with different substances by changing the attachment; in doing this, layers ranging from a few millimetres to several metres are possible.
    c   Different surface finishes can be achieved using various polishing attachments.

a   b   c

Forming processes

A distinction needs to be made between primary shaping and forming. In the case of primary shaping a plastic raw material, which has been released from its material cohesion, is formed into a semi-finished product such as a sheet. In the case of forming, on the other hand, the material cohesion of the raw material is retained. A first type of forming process is used in the manufacturing of semi-finished products e.g. flanged profiles. A further type of forming takes place as a subsequent processing step in which the original state of a semi-finished product (e.g. a profile) is modified. The result of this is an optimization of the original state, e.g. an improvement of the rigidity or the adaptation to a desired geometry. The volume of the component part before and after forming is the same. Forming processes are primarily used on metal and plastic materials, but also find application with wooden materials (e.g. bentwood) and mineral raw materials.

The forming processes can be illustrated using metallic semi-finished products as an example. In the case of cold forming the reforming takes place below re-crystallization temperature. In the case of warm forming, re-crystallization, that is a change in the molecular structure of the component part, occurs. The combination of both processes increases the cost-effectiveness, as the forming power needing to be used can be reduced.

Forming processes occur through mechanical pressure or tension which is exerted upon a component part. Under the umbrella terms pressure and tension forming we differentiate between rolling, free forming, die forming or deep-drawing, pressure forming, hydroforming, widening and tool-less wire drawing.

Forming can be differentiated along the lines of the prevailing bending strain, thus making it easily comprehensible for the designer. In the case of bend forming the tool is moved exclusively in a straight line. Free bending combines bending and straightening (bending by building up pressure at specific points), free circular form bending and transverse-force-free bending. In the case of die forming you have to use a tool, the so-called die: using this, circular form bending, beading, flanging and hydroform bending are possible. Particularly relevant for the architect are bend forming with a rotational tool movement and roll bending/roll shaping. These refer to linear forming processes which generate complexly formed integral construction parts.

Table T5 shows the standard industrial forming processes. The matrix differentiates between warm forming processes and cold forming processes. In warm forming processes, pressure or heat loosen the crystal structure of the material and in this way enable the material to be reformed more easily. In cold forming the reforming is brought about exclusively by mechanical pressure of friction on the material. In doing this it does not lead to a mineralogical alteration of the original material.

41 Steel sheet folded according to the programmed requirement
42 CNC-programmable swing-folding machine with a maximum component part breadth of 12 m

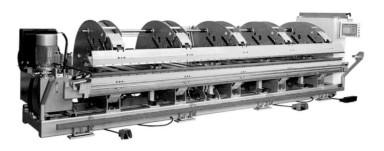

41

42

T5: Comparison of the most important forming processes (very different technologies – for most of them metal is suited as a raw material)

Technology	CNC punching	CNC folding	CNC bending	Hydroforming	Linear flow splitting	Flexible roll forming	Deep-drawing (Thermoforming)	Injection moulding
Symbol								
Construction material	Sheet steel, stainless sheet steel, sheet aluminium, cardboards, papers, textiles	Sheet steel, stainless sheet steel, sheet aluminium	Steel, stainless steel and aluminium hollow profiles/ pipes/sheets	Steel, stainless steel and aluminium hollow profiles/ pipes/sheets, magnesium/ titanium/nickel alloys	Steel, stainless steel and aluminium flat bar steel and U profiles	Steel, stainless steel and aluminium flat bar steel	Thermoplastic synthetic materials, acrylic glass, plexiglass, polycarbonates, Makrolon	Plastics, thermoplastic resins, elastomers and thermo-setting resins
Maximum construction size	4000 × 1625 mm	Folding length from 2000 to 6000 mm	Bending length: in theory limitless, dependent on the restrictions of the assembly hall and transport	1200 × 2000 mm	Dependent on the length of the processed band length	Dependent on the length of the processed band length	Dependent on the size of the available press, max. 5000 × 5000 mm	Dependent on the raw material and the manu-factured tool, max. 3000 × 3000 mm
Material thickness	Up to approx. 8 mm	Up to approx. 8 mm	Up to approx. 6 mm	Up to approx. 8 mm	Up to approx. 6 mm	Up to 30 mm	1–15 mm	5–30 mm
Accuracy	0.1 mm	Up to 0.2 mm	± 0.2 degrees	1 mm	2 mm	1 mm	0.5 mm	0.5 mm
Possibility of follow-up processing/ finishing	Not necessary, dependent on the use of the part, can be easily painted	Thread cutting, heading, thread bolting, weld nuts, surface protection	Not necessary	Not necessary	Deburring Grinding	Deburring Grinding	Not necessary	Not necessary (smoothing edges if at all)
Geometry data input	Accepts the usual data for-mats (parasolid, dxf, etc.)	Accepts the usual data formats (parasolid, dxf, etc.)	2D dxf, dwg 3D iges, step	Data for creating the negative form are needed	dxf, dwg	dxf, dwg	Data for creating the negative form are needed	Data for creating the negative form are needed
Manufacturer	MICRONORM Woronka GmbH	G.W.P. Manufacturing Services AG Thalmann Machinenbau AG	Manufacturers of long pipe bending machines G.W.P. Manufacturing Services AG	DAVI ZIETA (FIDU technology)	DAVI	Daimler	G.W.P. Manufacturing Services AG	Gregor Hofbauer GmbH
Use	Architecture, automotive industry, electronic appli-ance industry	Mechanical engineering, structural-facings sector, roofing industry	Architecture, furniture industry, mechanical engineering, plant construc-tion	Automotive industry, oil industry, heating, furniture industry, optics, household technology, pro-file processing	Supporting structures, automotive bodywork	Vehicle con-struction, me-chanical engi-neering, plant construction, construction industry, furni-ture industry	Power engi-neering, medical technology, furniture industry	Furniture industry, consumer goods industry, structural-facings sector

43

CNC bending edges

The bending of sheets (also called folding) takes place by folding the flat surface of a component over the remaining part of a sheet metal plate. The procedure is fully automated and the curved edge, angle and radius parameters are exactly defined and reproducible. The contraction of the curve when unrolling the sheet must be calculated as part of the planning. We differentiate between the following three folding processes.

Die bending

Actual folding is also called die bending; the corresponding machines are called press brakes or brake presses. Bending processes produce edges which are always straight. Bending a sheet 180° is called a fold-over. The process is primarily used for manufacturing cold profiles. The machine required for this consists of the upper tool (punch) and the lower tool (die) (fig. 44). The form of the component part in a 3-point bending process is determined by three exactly defined support points in the lower tool. Configuring the base of the die sets the programmed angle.

The die holder enables different dies, which vary in their breadth (7–90 mm) and their groove depth, to be interchanged easily. A sheet or strip is inserted into the machine, then the punch is lowered into the die and the sheet is transformed into the desired profile. Specific profile forms are defined by variations in the punch and die.

Swing folding

The sheet is clamped between an upper and lower cheek and folded through a swinging movement of the bending cheek. Alongside individual swing-folding machines there are bending centres used for the flexible production of large quantities of complex curved forms. Typical products are: housings, office furniture, doors and cartridges. By not using fixed dies, swing folding is significantly more flexible than die bending. Through CNC-controlled feeding of the sheet which is to be processed, it is also possible to execute folding processes which are not at right angles to one another.

Roll bending

The process is a special form of swing folding in which the bending cheek is moved away from the sheet in a controlled way during the swinging movement. This prevents relative movement between the tool and the sheet which avoids scratching the surface of the sheet. The process is well suited to bending stainless steel and sheets with a pre-coated surface.

CNC-controlled bending centres enable programmable bending radii and developable surface. Through a variable sheet feed, folded plates and conical supporting structures become possible. Restrictions lie mostly in the geometry created, which, from a certain size upwards, collides with the machine itself. The potential of the technique is being permanently developed further so that more complex bending forms are possible. With the simple principle of material forming the performance of sheet materials is increased considerably.

CNC-controlled bending

In general bending refers to the exertion of a bending moment on a material which, as a result, experiences a plastic transformation. In order to achieve these changes in form, the pressure must exceed the elasticity limit of the material. In the case of CNC-controlled bending, bending machines give materials and semi-finished products such as sheets,

43 Burg Giebichenstein University of Art and Design in Halle (D), Anderhalten Architekten; the cartridges made from gold-anodized 10-mm-thick aluminium sheets are all of a different size.
44 3-point bending machine which enables a variation in the degree of bending through interchangeable dies.
45 The swing-folding bending machine allows a variety of geometries to be created through a CNC-controlled feed. The sheet is guided, in a CNC-controlled way, between the upper and lower cheek, which fix it in position during the folding. The bending cheek bends the sheet to the desired angle.

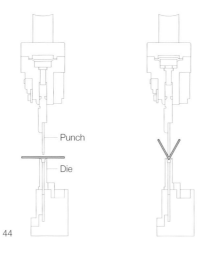

Punch

Die

44

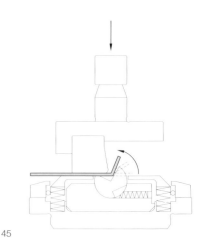

45

46

47

48

wires, bars and pipes a form which was digitally predefined. The principle has been around since the 1970s and since then is being continually optimized and simplified. The seamless integration of the digital design process rationalizes both serial production and individual production to the same degree and, in addition, reduces mistakes.

In construction it is mostly the free-form bending process which is used, i.e. a type of roll bending in which three or more bending rollers (fig. 49) transform the shape. The position of the bending rollers in relation to one another determines the bending radius. Decisive parameters for production are: type of material, thickness of material, hardness of material as well as the bending angle. The CNC programming of the process balances out the ability of the metal to reset itself by taking into account the exact parameters of the material being processed as part of the forming process.
The predefined bending angle is achieved to a 0.1° level of accuracy. The input program stores the bending definitions for repeat productions of the same component parts and for the correction of inputting errors.

The following benefits come to the fore in bending processes:
- The fibre orientation of the semi-finished part is not disturbed.
- Improvement in the strength of the component part through the change in geometry and re-crystallization of the material
- The possibility of creating complex 3D geometries
- Good dimensional and form accuracy
- No loss of material
- Cost-effective manufacturing in the case of both high and low numbers of units
- Varying sized bending radii can be bent continuously using one set of tools.
- Manufacturing of long construction elements without additional connections such as welded rivets or screws
- Good configuration options to cope with variations in batches
- Can be automated well.

CNC bending technology is used in architecture mainly for the production of sophisticated supporting structures. The number of costly welded joints is reduced, compared to construction with linear parts, resulting from the pre-form-

ing of the semi-finished products. The reduction of working steps leads to a quick production flow. Due to the direct data transfer and the possibility of bending various free forms with one set of tools, this process is worthwhile even with small numbers of units. At the design stage the following parameters should be considered:
- Each material/semi-finished product has a minimum bending radius.
- A decrease in the load-bearing capacity of profiles as a result of the formation of dents and folds is to be avoided.
- The possibilities for processing are dependent on capacity, e.g. size of the hall or machine, or of the company doing the processing.

46 Bent rolled section in the factory
47 Linearly bent tube profile
48 Bending process of a rolled section
49 Bending parameters with material characteristics and the expected reset force
50 CNC-controlled bending machine with roller actuators
   a Tube clamping function, pipe feeder, and automatic plane rotation
   b Mandrel bar with mandrel at the front end; length of the mandrel bar = maximum length of the tube
   c "Lever" arm to bend the tube

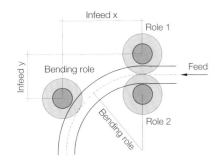

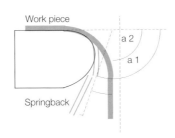

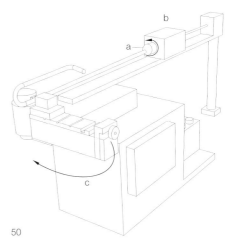

49

50

51

Basically we distinguish between two levels of complexity in bending. In the case of 2-axial bending almost all profiles can be used; the component part is bent on one plane. In the case of 3-axial bending the component part is transformed on two planes in a processing procedure and is curved in several directions. For 3-axial bending, tube shapes are above all suited due to the torsions which appear in the component part. In the case of right-angled profiles it is a case of denting the material along the level surfaces of the hollow profile. In bending processes which produce construction parts for further processing it is important that reference points are marked on the component parts using graining (a small indentation) to provide guidance for further processing. It is also necessary to code modular parts which are joined to make up a large form. The graining must define both the position of the tubular axle as well as potential welding points on the construction parts.

Many supporting structures feature multi-directional curves which can only be constructed with linear construction elements through triangulation (division into triangles). In order to realize geometries like

this in a more integral way there are two possibilities: on the one hand dividing the geometry up into 2-axial curved modular parts, which ultimately – rotated around their tubular axis – are welded together to create a multi-axial curved form, and on the other hand the immediate production of the multi-axial curved form in a bending process. Stipulations from the structural planning determine the geometry of the tube; increased requirements can be catered for by enlarging the wall thickness of the tube segment by segment. The advantage over modular geometry constructions is a high level of inherent rigidity through the curvature created.

It is not possible to realize a work of art, such as the "Angerpark Landmark" walk-in large-scale sculpture in Duisburg in the shape of a walk-in roller coaster, without CNC tube-bending technology. Each construction part is inherently geometrically different. The supporting tube with a diameter of 324 mm follows a multi-directional curvature over its 214 m length. Production takes place in modular segments with a length of approx. 14 m on a multi-axial large-format bending machine. The form of the sculpture is subject to the parameter limits which

determine the minimal bending radii of the main supporting tube.

CNC punching and nibbling
In this procedure a vertically movable punching tool with a high hydraulic pressure processes the base material sheet and in doing so changes its form. Since the 1980s punching machines have been controlled by computers. Either the tool travels over the material or the material travels under a stationary punching tool. The form of the punching depends on the tool on the punching head; new machines can change these punching tools automatically during the processing procedure.

There are three different processes:
· *Embossment punching*
  Here the surface of a component part is altered beyond its point of plastic distortion and thus is embossed or folded.
· *Punch cutting or nibbling*
  In this process the component part is separated along the punching edge. As the punching tool continually travels over the component part it can be used as blank cutting tool.
· *Rotational punching*
  Here, specific openings or threads are worked into the component part.

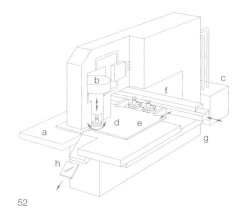

52

T6: Bending parameters of standard profile types

Profile types	Bending standard sizes			
	minimum		maximum	
	Profile	Bending radius	Profile	Bending radius
I and H profiles Light axis IPE/IPB	IPE 80 HE 100AA	50 mm	IPE 1000 HE 1000B	4000 mm
I and H profiles Heavy axis HE	IPE 80 HE 100AA	100 mm	IPE 600 HE 550A	5000 mm
U profiles Brackets to the outside/inside	30 × 33 × 5 mm	40 mm	UNP 400	2000 mm
U profiles Brackets to the outside	30 × 33 × 5 mm	50 mm	UNP 400	2000 mm
ROR tube profiles	21.3 t = 2.3 mm	30 mm	1219, t = 25 mm	On request

53

Alongside the standard tools, companies offer tools which are individually configured to the customer's requirements. As the costs for a special tool can be up to several thousand euros, it is only worth the expense at a correspondingly high component part production. Using these specialist tools, component parts can be given threading, beading for reinforcement and folds or plates on the same machine. Embossing and lettering tools can apply lettering and ornamentation. Only the size of the component part and the machine restrict the scope of the design. Processing curved surfaces is only possible in a limited way and at a high economic cost. There are machines which have both a punching head and a laser head so that both processes can be carried out on one machine in order to further automate production.

In the realization of the Unesco Forum in Barcelona by Herzog & de Meuron, CNC-punched and embossed sheets clad the building. The idea was to design the roof to give the impression of reflections in water. To this end the picture of a real water surface was translated into a vector graphic using Photoshop, which defines the route of travel

of the punching machine for texturing the sheet.

In the course of a year the contractor produced 28,000 triangular sheet panels with a continuous embossed pattern. None of the 0.8-mm-thick stainless steel panels with an edge length of approx. 1.10 m is the same as the others. At selected places the embossed pattern becomes a perforation and serves to ventilate the area behind the façade. Each triangle is unique but as a result of the parametric production technology this aspect does not cause any additional costs. Coding on the façade panels precisely defines the specific assembly location. Although the usage described is primarily ornamental it contributes to the stabilization of the surfaces through the plastic deformation of the thin sheets.

The machine used can process sheet steel, stainless steel and aluminium from 0.5 to 0.8 mm. The maximum working area is 3070 x 1660 mm with a punching force of 220 kN. This produces 1000 punching/2800 lettering processes per hour to an accuracy of 0.1 mm. Rotation takes place on the x- and y-axis and the machine can incorporate up to 21 different tools.

51 Angerpark Landmark, Duisburg (D), a project of the European capital of culture RUHR.2010 in partnership with Sonja Becker + Rüdiger Karzel, bk2a architektur/Cologne; Arnold Walz, Parametric 3 D Planning, designtoproduction/Stuttgart; ifb frohloff staffa kühl ecker/Berlin; the complex roller coaster forms can only be realized with fully parameterized design and production.
52 CNC punching machine
  a Machine bench
  b Plunger
  c Hydraulic assembly
  d Tool rotation
  e Sheet plate
  f Tools
  g Clamping shoes
  h Tool
53 Punched stainless steel sheet cladding, Forum Barcelona (E) 2005, Herzog & de Meuron
54 Graphical transformation of a photograph of water into a dot matrix using Photoshop
55 Assembled façade panels which transmit the impression of water into the physical space

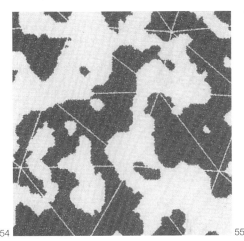

54

55

56

Pressure forming

Alongside folding and bending, pressure forming is the third relevant process for transforming sheet materials. For pressure forming, plastically distortable materials such as sheet steel or steel semi-finished products are used. Under the generic term hydroforming we distinguish between external high-pressure forming and internal high-pressure forming. Both processes are among the active-medium-based forming processes in which an emulsion of water and oil is used as the active medium for pressure. In both processes a press is used which generates a force ranging between 3000 and 50 000 kN. These forces are required in order to fix and distort the sheet during the transformation process.

In external high-pressure forming, a sheet is clamped above a water pressure tank and pre-formed or bulged out using hydraulic pressure. As soon as the sheet is in a fluid state the actual forming process begins whereby a punch presses the sheet into a water tank. With the increase of pressure in the water tank the construction part is fully stamped in its form. The transformed sheet has a very smooth surface as there is no contact with a solid body. In the case of smaller construction parts with less requirement for precision, a purely hydraulic external high-pressure forming process is used. Here the component part is pressed into its form purely using the active medium without using a negative mould to create the form.

In the case of internal high-pressure forming, closed hollow cross-sections such as tubes are distended into an all-round hollow form under a pressure of up to 4000 bar. Tearing of the raw material is prevented by additional mechanical compression and repositioning of the material. The punches are designed as

hollow forms through the front sides of which the tube is filled with the pressure medium after which the required internal pressure is built up. Through this process, very exact and light construction parts with complex geometries and high stability are created in one operation. The advantages over other formation processes are fewer individual parts, a high level of accuracy in terms of form and scale and hence a high level of stability and low weight.

Aluminium, brass, copper, cold or hot rolled steel, stainless steel, magnesium, titanium and nickel alloys are all suitable for hydroforming. Both internal and external high-pressure forming require the production of a negative form, the so-called mould or die, which is why these procedures are only suitable for large series and are not economical for small batches. Areas of use include complex joint hubs in lightweight construction as well as multi-directionally curved, repetitive façade elements.
As hydroformed construction parts are produced in one operation, without welded seams or other types of joins, they are superior to traditional procedures. This is a method for forming sheet material which is extremely suited to the material involved.

Free internal pressure forming

The so-called free internal pressure forming process was developed at ETH Zurich (professor's chair in CAAD, Prof. Ludgar Hovestadt) by Oskar Zieta and Philipp Dohmen.
It enables the production of closed, non-linear and complex hollow bodies from sheet material. Forming processes such as, for example, folding and bulging, make sheet metal into an extremely resistant form. The material behaves in a similar way to arching a piece of paper

which is only stable when you deform it. Comparable with internal and external high-pressure forming, in the free internal pressure forming procedure, sheets of material are formed under high pressure, which means that the material is "inflated".
The free internal pressure forming method has the advantage of allowing sheet metal to be processed without tools; production of unique pieces becomes possible. Two sheets of metal are welded together in an airtight way along a defined digital path. The final forming of the sheets takes place via the introduction of water or air pressure into the hollow space. The internal pressure determines to what extent the sheets are deformed.
After the forming medium has drained off a stable form is the result. The geometry of the layout (contour) and the internal pressure determine the final design.

In the first stage of the process, a laser cuts out the contours of the metal sheets. Here, a 3–5 mm overlapping edge must remain for the welding process which follows. The two sheets, which are lying on top of one another, are welded together by a robot, whose movements are either controlled by a computer or manually guided (see "Jointed-arm robotics", p. 61). The deformation of the welded contours takes place using a pressure of 6 to 50 bar depending on the size of the construction parts. While material consumption stays the same the forms generated in this way are many times more stable than comparable forms made from folded sheets. In static load tests, static projections are far exceeded. This method of processing sheet metal extends the freedoms of laser welding and cutting to the forming process. The result is an individual language of form which we do not normally associate with sheet metal. As a result of this, in architecture, new perspectives open up for sheet metal as a basic material. The process is well suited to the type of materials in question and uses the potential of its inherent rigidity after forming. Whereas for steel profiles there are standardized construction tables, for static projections of the load-bearing capacity of complex sheet metal constructions the so-called finite element methods are needed.

The long-term goal is to transform sheet metals precisely cut and welded by laser into light, high-quality and stable architectonic constructions such as supporting structures or façade construction parts.

56 Two sheet metals, which have been welded one on the top of the other in an airtight way, are literally inflated.
57 At the Architonic exhibition stand for IMM 2010 in Cologne a structure resembling a supporting structure is realized for the first time using the free internal pressure forming process (design: Oskar Zieta).

57

Project examples of digital processes

74   The Sphere at Deutsche Bank in Frankfurt
Mario Bellini Architects, Milan,
with Bollinger+Grohmann Engineers,
Frankfurt am Main

76   Pedestrian bridge in Reden
FloSundK Architects, Saarbrücken,
with Bollinger+Grohmann Engineers,
Frankfurt am Main

77   Rolex Learning Center in Lausanne
SANAA Architects, Tokyo,
with Bollinger+Grohmann Engineers,
Frankfurt am Main

82   Hungerburg funicular in Innsbruck
Zaha Hadid Architects, London,
with Bollinger + Grohmann Engineers,
Frankfurt am Main

86   National Temple of Divine Providence
in Warsaw
Szymborski & Szymborski Architects

92   Taichung Metropolitan Opera House
in Taiwan
Toyo Ito & Associates, Architects, Tokyo,
with Arup, London

Above a certain level of complexity,
construction processes can only proceed in an interdisciplinary, simultaneous,
integrative and computer-aided way.
Six practical examples illustrate how digital processes support the design and
execution of sophisticated buildings.

The projects shown embody the character of division of labour which is determined by the close cooperation between
specialist engineers and the architect.
Digital planning technology is the construction communication of the 21st century which is developing a new architectural language. Constructions are being
created which no longer only stem from
a fascination with digital forms but rather
follow an algorithmically generated logic.
Innovative production technologies facilitate the efficient execution of this intelligent architecture.

Digital generation of a supporting structure

In most phases, the design process for supporting structures is permeated by digital technologies. Computer-based working almost always means an optimization of previous processes as the computer automates repetitive operations and by this means can provide a high level of precision. Furthermore, design-related paradigms change when digital techniques are being used conceptually and comprehensively. In the following, the conceptual application of computer-based methods in early design phases is illustrated using a series of projects as examples. Computers can generate and evaluate many design variants and thus identify previously unknown solutions. Supporting structures are generated, immediately evaluated and adapted to specific situations.

Parametric models
Two-dimensional and three-dimensional computer models can be significantly more than just a more precise form of drawing-based representation. Each point, each curve, each surface which is generated using a modelling program, and is thus mathematically described, requires input parameters. A point is based on x-, y- and z-coordinates, the line on its start and end point, or on start point, directional vector and length. Parametric modelling software is capable of storing this formation process so that the historical basis of the development of each individual object is known. Objects can be built up on one another. In this way points lie on a plane in a space, a line is based on exactly these points, and in turn surfaces are based on a host of lines. These associations are retained beyond the process of generation. A hierarchical structure of interdependencies,

a type of living geometry is created. To show the relationships between the objects the image of the parent/child relationship is often used. If you stay with this analogy then parametric software applications enable you to travel in time: if you change the input parameters of a parent object then this has an effect on all its children. A working procedure like this can occur at any time. Thus, a few simple input parameters can guide a parametric model with complex hierarchies and interdependencies. If these parameters are not set with fixed values but rather are variable, then, by manipulating them, a multitude of geometrically different variations can be generated. So when using parametric software, alongside the finished object, you design and describe its formation process and through this a parametric spectrum of possible solutions. Instead of an individual solution you get a range of many possible solutions.

If you use this approach for generating supporting structures, then, for example, the number of diagonal members in a trussed girder can be parametrically described. In addition, if the input parameters determine which joint hub on the top boom is connected with which joint hub on the bottom boom, then a new topology can be generated. If the solution space is designed in a sensible way, supporting structures may be created which cannot be assigned to any known topology.

Analysis
The generation of parametric supporting structures is followed by their analysis. A new type of supporting structure is only worthwhile if it spans further than traditional supporting structures, needs less material or answers to specific architectural demands. The geometry of parametric models is expected to describe a

cohesive system which reacts to external forces and transfers loads into the building ground. If you follow the logic of large solution spaces then these are first reviewed in their entirety and not designed as a single solution and further developed step by step. This means that a lot of results, which are initially based on random input parameters, are generated and analyzed. This initial rough analysis must take place automatically, as proceeding manually with the large number of solutions would be too costly. Software applications for analyzing supporting structures are able to calculate even very complex support systems. So a supporting structure design does not necessarily need to be broken down into its constituent parts in order to evaluate it. Instead, the overall system with all its elements and their interactions is examined. To do this, an initial interface between geometry generation and analysis is needed, which automatically transfers the data. At this point working digitally makes full use of the pure calculative capacity of the computer.

If we stay with the example of the parametric trussed girder then the geometry model describes the axes of the steel profiles which meet at common start and end points. For the analysis of the supporting structure the lines need to be translated into joint hubs and connecting elements and finally given cross-sections, material characteristics, bearings and loading conditions.

The most important loading conditions, for example, vertical loads in the case of bridges and horizontal loads in the case of towers, are examined. In doing this, each model within the solution space will provide different parameters for distortion, maximum torques and tensions. If all the models are analyzed then a ranking list of good and less good supporting structures can be created.

Circularity and feedback loop
Analysis software can play an important generative role in design if the results of an analysis are used as a guiding instruction for the subsequent working step, in other words as feedback. As early as in the 1940s, cybernetics, which is concerned with technical and biological control and regulation systems, described the concept of circularity and feedback loops: a system within an environment perceives external conditions and in line with this examines which actions are necessary in order to reach a particular goal. These actions alter the external condition and also the relationship of the system and the environment. This altered condition is once again perceived by the system and the same process happens again. In the same way, the helmsman (Greek: kybernétes) of a ship steers towards a port and continually corrects the course of the ship which has deviated from the ideal course due to the wind and waves.

The concept of circularity has become technical and digital reality with the computer. Parametric models are being constantly checked in continuous loops, imperceptibly to the user, for alterations in their input parameters. Only these updating cycles allow us an interaction with a model like this and its parameters running in real time. If you apply the principle of circularity and feedback loops in the design process then supporting structure designs can be developed in an iterative process. The solution space is reviewed and the best solutions serve as the input parameters for the next iteration.

Evolving designs
Evolutionary algorithms take advantage of these principles. They imitate processes we find in natural evolution, which is why you will also find terms in the language used to talk about this subject which you know from evolutionary theory. An initially random population of solutions, widely distributed across the solution space, is evaluated and arranged into a ranking list according to their fitness for purpose. The fitness for purpose of an individual solution is measured against previously defined evaluation criteria, which may be relevant to the supporting structure, but may also be based on architectonic criteria, in as much as these are quantifiable. In the subsequent iteration, the genetic material – in other words the parameters, which guide the model – of the best solutions is combined again so that offspring are created, which are based on the parameters of the "fit" individuals of a population. New combinations (crossovers) of parameters and mutation (small, chance alterations to variables) provide variation. The evaluation of the individuals is taken over by fitness functions. If the process runs over several generations, solutions develop which adapt to the previously defined criteria. Here, variation takes place randomly and in an untargeted way. So the correct developmental direction, as well as the selection of good solutions, is once again guided by the fitness functions.

Digital tools and processes enable this way of working as large quantities of data can be generated, analyzed and altered automatically. The results do not follow any predefined typologies but rather are specific solutions developed for the context in hand.
Although an algorithm is inherently an extremely formalized system of unequivocal guidance directions whose mode of operating is completely transparent, supporting structures still result, which would not have been discovered without this development process. The process of coming into being plays a central role and cannot be skipped. Multiple or even contradictory evaluation criteria can be used. An evolutionary algorithm can identify the solutions with the best balance of all requirements.

When using the procedures described, a large proportion of the design work is focused on the definition of basic conditions, fitness criteria and solution spaces. The process of coming into being withdraws itself from being directly controlled. Exactly this transfer of control, however, allows established patterns of thought and technical solutions to be overcome. Reviewing very large solution spaces requires a high level of computational power and can also be time-consuming. However, assuming the development of hardware to date, the possibilities will continue to expand so that in the future the spectrum of evaluation criteria will also be larger. The goal is solutions which combine architectonic criteria, criteria relevant to the supporting structure, and ecological criteria in a balanced relationship. The examples introduced in the following chapters should illustrate what is already possible today.

Klaus Bollinger,
Manfred Grohmann, Oliver Tessmann

The Sphere at Deutsche Bank in Frankfurt

Architect: Mario Bellini Architects, Milan
Digital design: Bollinger + Grohmann,
                    Frankfurt am Main
Structural design: Bollinger + Grohmann,
                    Frankfurt am Main
Completion: anticipated for 2010

For the foyer of the new headquarter of the Deutsche Bank in Frankfurt, the Milan-based architect Mario Bellini designed a sculpture which resembles a ball wrapped in ribbons. Two bridges which are inserted through this sphere connect both towers of the bank. A series of rings, with varying radii, is positioned on the virtual surface of the sphere. The arrangement of the rings is supposed to express the liberty of the chosen concept without the need of additional supporting structures.

In the first stage of the design, sixty circles were generated which were all defined by three points on the surface of the sphere. The attribution of the circles to the sphere is controlled by a genetic algorithm. In the first step sixty circles are generated. Subsequently they are arranged through an iterative process respecting the defined parameters. The large number of rings automatically results in intersections, thus creating a stable spatial network.

The genetic algorithm is used to find the exact solution which forms an effective supporting structure with an even distribution of rings and without cutting through the bridges. The genome, in other words the parameters for the coordination of the rings on the sphere, is saved as a binary character string. In a 3D modelling program, which can be controlled using scripting (user programming, see p. 24f.), geometric models of 50 different individual spheres of one generation are created from this string. The circles of each individual are then divided into traverses. In the support structure model, the intersection points of the circles and subdivisions of the curved parts which lie between them form joint hubs and connecting member elements. Transferred into construction this means

1

74

2

that all joint hubs within a building are defined as bearings. The flat steel profiles of the rings are oriented towards the corresponding centre point of each circle. This support structure model is now examined with a view to its distortion under its own weight. In addition, a collision check is carried out on the rings and the clearance profile of the bridge as well as an analysis of the position of the circle levels. A good solution is characterized by the following criteria:

• Minimal distortion of the supporting system
• Little or no penetration of the clearance profile of the bridge
• Large angles between the circle levels and hence an even distribution of the rings

The best support structure solution would result from spanning the curved parts between the bearings. However, this type

of configuration would contain a lot of rings at similar levels so that, due to the almost parallel arrangement, it would lead to an uneven distribution of the rings. However, as the genetic algorithm evaluates the fitness of each individual sphere on the basis of all criteria simultaneously, solutions emerge which fulfil all requirements and create a balance between them. In each evaluation process, the individuals are selected from the ranking list created upon whose genetic information the following generation is based. For the selection from all of the results there are various procedures, by which not only the fittest individuals survive; even solutions which have been evaluated as bad have a chance to pass on their genetic material. This way of proceeding makes sure there is a large spectrum of variants and prevents a local optimum being identified as the supposed best solution.

The final solution found for the sphere fulfilled all of the three required criteria – therefore the development process was ended. Alongside the original design idea from the competition, the criteria relevant to the supporting structure could be introduced and become an integrative part of the design.

Klaus Bollinger,
Manfred Grohmann, Oliver Tessmann

1   Competition rendering
2   Mock-up of a joint hub where the rings intersect
3   Mutation of intersections; gradual improvement procedure
4   Digital analysis model

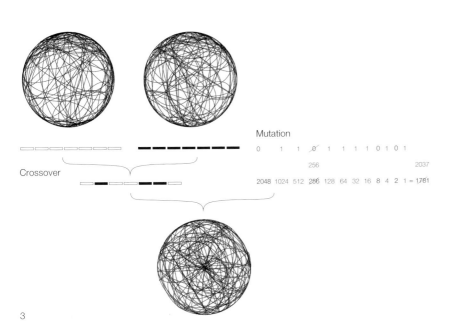

3

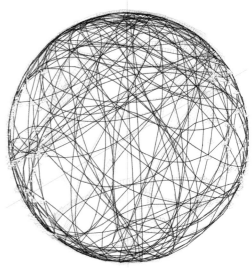

4

Pedestrian bridge in Reden

Architect: FloSundK, Saarbrücken
Digital design: Bollinger + Grohmann,
                 Frankfurt am Main
Competition: 2007

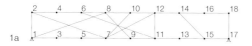

1a

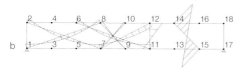

b

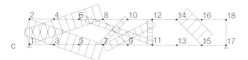

c

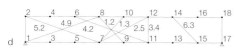

d

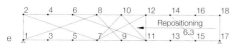

e

As part of a competition for a pedestrian bridge over a railway line and gardens in Reden (Saarland) the engineers, together with the architects, designed a bridge support structure. Its exact topology was developed using an evolutionary process.

The bridge support structure consists of two trussed girders which initially both stand upright. In the direction of the garden they turn gradually more outwards thus leaving the view of the country park open. The thickness of the members was also to decrease gradually with the increasing rotation of the girders as well as opening out. This meant the external contour of the girders was set, whereas the connecting diagonals could be arranged freely. For this stage of the work a parametric model was developed which enabled random distribution of members along the top and bottom boom. The emerging supporting structure was calculated and each individual diagonal evaluated. This evaluation was based on the fact that in a truss each diagonal must be stressed to normal force without bending moments occurring. Therefore the ratio of moment and normal force can be seen

as an indicator of the fitness of the individual diagonals.

Subsequently an iterative procedure identified members with an unfavourable bending moment/normal force relationship as individuals with poor fitness. As they were not desired to be part of the next generation they were shifted to new positions. The altered structure was then evaluated again so that a continual improvement of the system ensued in the development process. The pedestrian bridge with its special requirements is based on a system which integrates and updates the design idea and thus enables an efficient solution.

Klaus Bollinger,
Manfred Grohmann, Oliver Tessmann

1   Process diagram of the supporting structure
    generation
    a Random distribution of members
    b Analysis of the bending moments
    c Analysis of the normal forces
    d Establishing fitness (bending moments/normal
       forces)
    e Identification of the most unfavourable member
       and its repositioning
2   Evolutionary steps of the overall supporting
    structure of the bridge from first design through
    to optimized structure; the structure gradually
    condenses on the bearings.

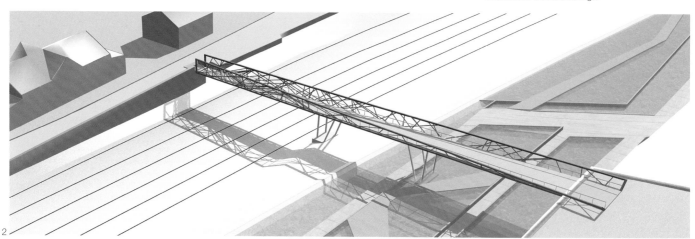

2

Rolex Learning Center in Lausanne

Architects:	SANAA Kazuyo Sejima & Ryue Nishizawa, Tokyo
Structural design:	Bollinger + Grohmann, Frankfurt am Main Walther Mory Maier Bauingenieure AG, Münchenstein, Switzerland INGPHI SA, Lausanne, Switzerland
Consultant engineering firm (preliminary designs):	SAPS Sasaki and Partners, Tokyo
General contractors:	Losinger Construction AG, Bussigny, Switzerland
3D consulting:	DesignToProduction
Completion:	2010

The Rolex Learning Center on the campus of the École Polytechnique Fédérale de Lausanne (EPFL) is based on a landscaped foundation slab, which generates the most varied spatial situations through a kind of artificial topography. The building, with its area of 166 × 121 m with a central library, study rooms, facilities and services for the acquisition of knowledge along with exhibition rooms, conference halls, a cafeteria and a restaurant, is intended to be the focal point of campus life and has a decisive effect on the appearance of the campus. The reinforced concrete foundation slab and the membrane roof with a substructure made of steel and glued laminated timber beams flow up and down in waves of up to 30° of incline. A homogenous perfect shell transfers the forces without bending stresses and can therefore be extremely thin. However, even introducing a door opening into such a perfect form can cause structural and formal problems. SANAA's landscape integrates around 14 patios with diameters of 7–50 m, creates visual relationships and the most varied spatial qualities and results from a design process in which considerations regarding the supporting structure were just one aspect amongst many others.

The task for the structural engineers was to discover the local shell and arch impact within the master geometry as well as carefully modifying it in close cooperation with the architects. Identifying qualities in an existing structure replaced the form-finding process. The load-bearing behaviour of a landscape like this is varied so there are no areas which represent a single type of supporting structure. Several analyses also revealed weak points within the geometry which would have meant a disproportional dimensioning of the concrete shell. The snake-like course of the forces within the membrane, high bending moments and deviation forces along with a lack of bearings in the patio areas made a reworking necessary. By shrinking and displacing the patios, it was possible to ensure that forces between the edges of the shell flowed in straight lines. This modification of the overall form and the position of several patios took place in close cooperation with the architects in an iterative process which lasted throughout the whole design period.

1   View of the roof landscape with the cut-out patios

1

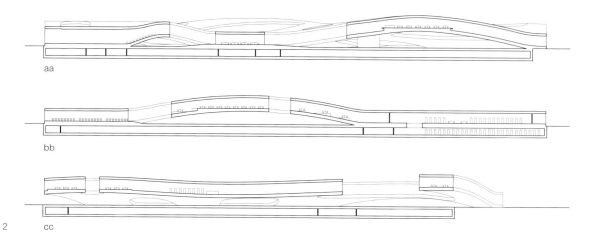

aa

bb

2   cc

During the competition and the first design phases the architects developed the geometry using physical models. Similar to a topographical model, the various heights were represented in layers. The first 3D models were based on the architects' contour models which were transitioned into continuous digital surface models. Surfaces like this have two dimensions which unfold in space straight or curved, limited or limitless. At the same time the geometry describes each point contained using x-, y- and z-coordinates in three dimensions. An object represented in this way does not lie inside or outside of a limitation but is the limitation itself. In the digital world this contradiction is not problematic. In the modelling program the surface can be manipulated directly or via a control polygon associated with it, and is tangible and controllable. Textures simulate materials and depth and allow the surfaces to appear as objects. However, if they are to be transitioned into built reality then the contradiction of surface and volume must be overcome. A type of bi-axial coordinate system makes it possible to unequivocally identify points, curves, bends and directional vectors at each point of the surface. This information can be used to arrange constructive elements. The surface now serves as a representation of a three-dimensional large-scale form and at the same time as a guiding geometry for a constructive system. For the structural design, digital surface models were needed in order to, for example, quickly and precisely generate and analyze vertical sections. They were used for the first rough analyses with the aid of the finite element method in which the surface is transformed into a network of finely dispersed meshes.

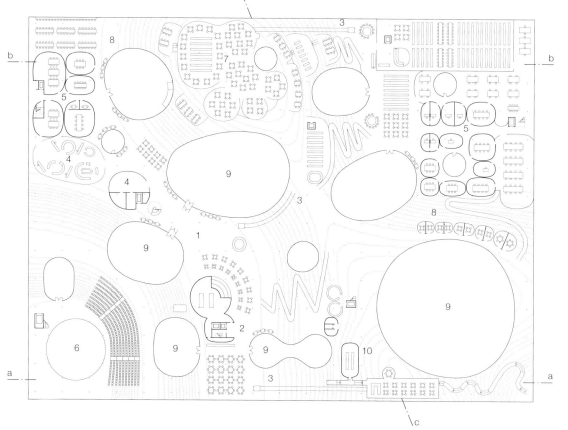

1   Main entrance
2   Café, bar, canteen
3   Inclined lift
4   Bank, bookshop
5   Offices
6   Multi-functional area
7   Library terraces
8   Work places
9   Patio
10 Restaurant, lake view

3

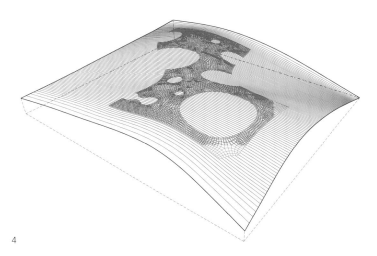

4

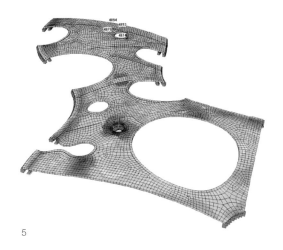

5

The computed results were manually checked again and again in parallel using simple 2D models and calculations. From these early analyses it was possible to determine initial criteria for the geometry, which were then used for the design in close cooperation with the architects:
- Adaptation of the location and position of the patios in such a way that load-removing arches can be spanned between them
- Optimization of the arch geometry in terms of symmetry and as parabolic a form as possible

- Avoidance of counter-curvature at the bearings which has an unfavourable effect on the load-bearing behaviour.

The support structure concept developed from this is based on a series of load-removing arches as the primary supporting structure and so-called ceiling zones which span between these arches. There are bending loads in all areas, unlike with pure shell support structures.
When calculating the system, three aspects were decisive: the confirmation of sufficient cross-section sizes under the loads acting on them, distortion and

2 Sections, scale 1:1200
3 Ground plan, scale 1:1200
4 Superimposition of surface model and finite element network
5 Visualization of the tension distribution in the shell
6 Position of the supporting arches in sections and as a ground plan

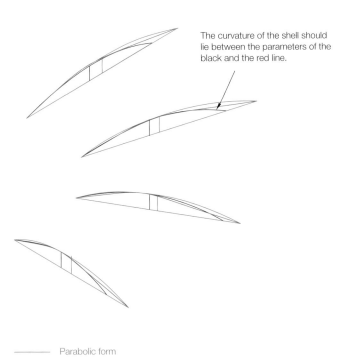

The curvature of the shell should lie between the parameters of the black and the red line.

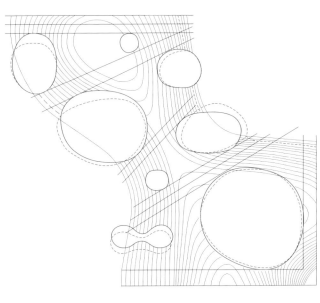

——— Parabolic form
——— Original form of the shell
——— Parabolic form retaining the position of maximum curvature

Patios and boundary

——— Solution 27 May 2006
Basis for the calculation
- - - - - Suggested alteration 06 June 2006

6

stability. These parameters were examined in a finite element software environment under the influence of crack formation, creeping and contraction of the concrete over an extended period.

The results from these analyses were transferred again and again into three-dimensional surface models. This step was necessary as the finite element networks often represent the geometry in an abstracted way and therefore make a precise formal architectonic evaluation impossible.

In the following phases, the exact geometrical description of the landscape served as a basis for the construction planning and ultimately for the implementation of the project. Even at an early stage the design team worked closely with the general building contractor. Due to the complexity of the task, the boundaries between support structure design and workshop planning could not be clearly drawn. The planning process relied on a continuous digital chain between geometric resolution and the subsequent generation of the working drawings. The details which a formwork plan needed to contain, so that the formwork construction and reinforcement could be carried out, could not be derived from standard procedures. The three-dimensional surface model served as the basis for the formwork construction. Two-dimensional drawings did not prove effective in this case. Nevertheless, a series of coordinates were made available in the form of plans. In a 50 × 50 cm grid, a set of plans gave details of the z coordinate, in other words, the respective height and local thickness of the concrete shell. A second set of plans provided the xy coordinates of the bearings, patio edges and zones of varying slab thicknesses. This information

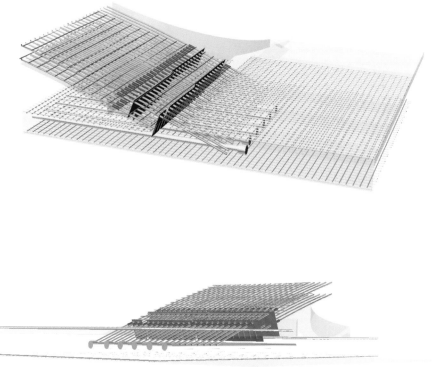

7

8

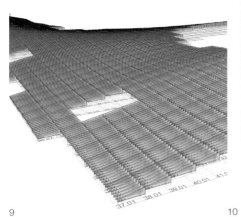

9   10   11

provided the basis for the calibration of the formwork benches in alignment with an on-site measurement. The generation of the plan could be automatically derived from the 3D models using macro-scripting. Scripting, a simplified form of programming, allows large amounts of repetitive modelling work to be automated and rule-based tasks to be processed and evaluated efficiently. Alongside time savings and a high degree of accuracy, the reduction of monotonous work (and hence susceptible to error) was an advantage of automation. The prefabricated formwork

consists of a series of 2.5 × 2.5 m benches, whose surfaces follow the course of the curvature of the landscape to be concreted. Each bench is made up of two wooden beams and an array of seven wooden ribs which lie on top of it. A laminated pulpwood board forms the surface. The contour form of the wooden ribs defines the geometry of the formwork. The generation of its geometry and subsequent translation into tool paths for the computer-controlled blank cutting of the ribs could be automated and thus speeded up a lot.
The experience from this and other

projects with complex three-dimensional geometry show that the 2D plan – which has been the standard design tool up until now – is increasingly losing in significance faced with pure 3D planning.

Klaus Bollinger,
Manfred Grohmann, Oliver Tessmann

7   Automated listing of coordinates
8   3D reinforcement bearing
9   Constructive 3D model of the formwork
10   Formwork bench consisting of two main beams, seven wooden ribs and a laminated pulpwood board
11   Formwork benches in use
12   Rendering

12

81

Hungerburg funicular in Innsbruck

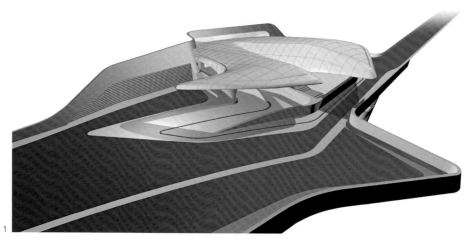

1

Architects: Zaha Hadid Architects, London
Thomas Vietzke (Project architect),
Jens Borstelmann, Markus Planteu
(Design team)

Structural design
Roof: Bollinger + Grohmann, Frankfurt
Arne Hoffmann (digital design),
Matthias Stracke (supporting
structure), Holger Techen (glass)

Completion: 2007

The new funicular railway connects the old town of Innsbruck with the district of Hungerburg and its continuation of transports visitors as far as the mountains of the Nordkette. For the four stops of the railway Zaha Hadid Architects developed a family of stations, which vary in geometry, but are all made of a plastically modelled concrete base and a free-form glass roof shell. Each station responds to its urban environment and the local topography. The development of adequate supporting structures and constructions was carried out in close cooperation with architects, structural engineers and contractors on the basis of digital surface area models. Plans and drawings only played a low-level role in this collaborative process. Many aspects of the design could only be communicated three-dimensionally and would have become unintelligible in two-dimensional projections. For example, computer-controlled blank cutting procedures need tool paths to be numerically specified, which means that the geometry is turned into a list of coordinates for guiding the tool and ultimately into the finished object.

The overall steel support structure was three-dimensionally modelled, transferred into finite element models for support structure analysis, and examined as a framework model (fig. 2). This major abstraction step simplified the calculations and yet leading to meaningful results. Thus, the support structure model is a derivation of the architectural model. The expert knowledge of the engineer when forming the model, and the focus on particular problem areas, is of decisive importance here. The load-bearing structure of the station roofs is made of 8–12 cm thick metal sheets which are arranged in a 1.25 m grid and follow the form of the external shell with a constant gap of 60 mm. Additional

lengthways ribs turn the system into a support grid. Only the bearing points penetrate the glass shell and are anchored in concrete. Therefore, individual, very high steel ribs had to be examined in detail as a surface model as the danger of buckling and distortion grows with increased height. In addition, the 3D model served as a basis for the computer-controlled production of the steel construction parts (fig. 3). The curved outlines of the ribs were extracted and transformed into fine resolution traverses (fig. 4). The position of all elements that connect with the construction part, such as bracing sheets, drip moulding, cross ribs and openings for screws, were also marked with circles. The outline and the holes, which served as precise markings during assembly on site, could then be cut in one working step. Information on coordinates and connecting points was engraved directly onto each construction part in order to indicate the assembly situation unequivocally.

Only glass could be employed as a material for the shell. The demands in terms of fire prevention, thermal resilience and surface quality made using glass-fibre reinforced plastics or acrylic glass impossible. As each of the glass panels is a two-directionally curved, unique, individual mould, components had to be made from a host of bent steel tubes. The production of each of the panels required two pieces of glass: the first piece of glass was heated and bent over the steel tubes and then served as the substructure for the façade element formed in the second phase.

A 3D model served as the basis for the mould construction. Following production, each panel was examined with a laser scanner and compared with the original geometry. This process of comparison of

1   Hungerburg station
2   FEM model, stability figure
3   3D model steel construction
4   Visualization of the tool paths for creating the
     steel ribs
5   Stations of the Hungerburg funicular
     a   Alpenzoo station
     b   Kongress station
     c   Löwenhaus station

2

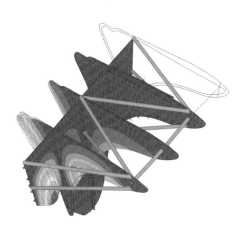

3

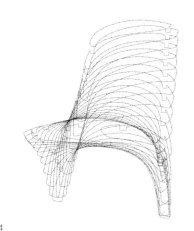

4

digital and physical reality is an important, constantly recurring working step. When connecting the two-directionally curved glass panes of the external shell with the load-bearing steel ribs beneath them, the differences between industrial and digital approaches become clear (fig. 7, p. 84).

In 1959 Konrad Wachsmann describes the principle of industrialization as "identical to the concept of mass production". [1] The fully automated factory is only "economically viable" through the production of "a large number of identical parts". This principle differentiates the factory from the workshop and alters the meaning of the term tool, which is no longer a general aid for a variety of tasks, but rather a specific moulding, punching or cutting device in a machine. Thus the forming tool is the only original in the production process and indirectly also the finished product. Each instance of the product is then just a copy. The mass product of series production always has to follow an abstract modular system of coordinates and through this can be combined without restriction. The ordering principle which goes with this is described by Wachsmann as modular coordination with reference to points, lines, planes and bodies. Each individual part within the system is clearly determined in relation to itself and in its relationship with all other parts. [2] If this logic of industrial construction is implemented, then, on the one hand, reliable and reproducible quality results, however, on the other hand, only that which conforms to this system can be built and become reality. Industrialization "cannot be misused as an aid for realizing freely devised conceptions. It can only be understood as the direct cause for the determination of the development of a particular product which determines the form of expression as a component or

5a

b

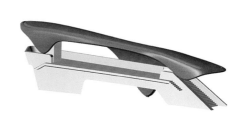

c

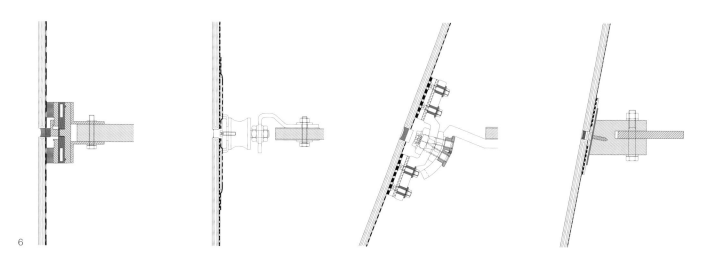

6

in combinations with others". [3] This rigorous approach is the foundation stone for many technical developments like the Mero joint and the furniture and architectural systems of Wachsmann's pupil Fritz Haller. [4]

Only a systematic approach as defined by Konrad Wachsmann, which cohesively correlates geometric coordination, automation and production technologies, could solve the problem with acceptable cost and time expenditure. In doing this the new degrees of freedom provided by digital technologies played an important role. In the design phase with the contractor, a repetitive process was

developed which produced serially differentiated construction parts. The potential of differentiation within the series, however, can only be taken advantage of if all phases from design to implementation are connected to one another by a seamless digital process chain. Of course, "the machine doesn't care" if it is cutting a curve or a straight line, but the generation of geometry, the logistics of the identification of construction parts, assembly processes and material consumption must also become part of the new system. The continuous digital workflow has the same elements which Wachsmann already

described and analyzed in his research; they just need to be adapted to the new technological possibilities. [5] The reference system for the glass holders (fig. 6) is the complex curved shell surface defined by the architects, which determines the contours of the steel ribs. A slotted polythene profile sits on the steel ribs (fig. 7) and with the exterior-facing surface follows the course of curvature of the glass shell geometry. The element is repeated in line with the rhythm of the distance between the ribs and at the same time adapts to the local curves of the reference geometry. In the design process a serial approach was initially

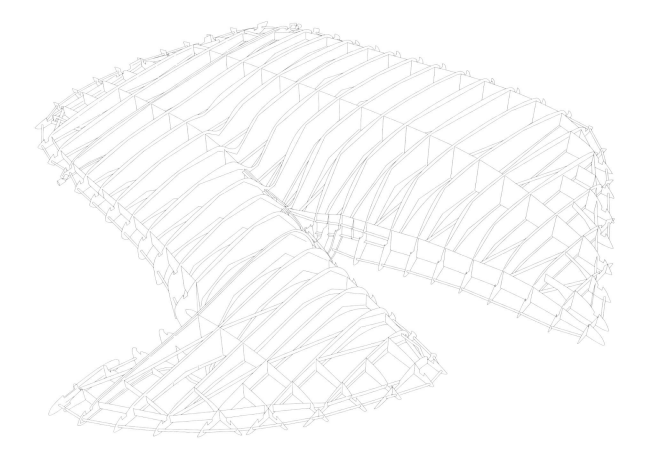

7

8

6 Development stages of the details of the glass
holders: step by step simplification of the adjusta-
ble articulated joint to form a mounting bracket
with stainless steel sheet and polythene profile
7 Isometry of the steel rib roof support structure
8 Curved glass panes in a moulding tool
9 View of roof from underneath – Hungerburg
funicular

used for the mounting of the glass panes: a standard articulated joint was to be aligned on the shell geometry during assembly. However, the cost of this adjustment would have quickly cancelled out the economic and temporal advantages of series production. The polythene profile, which is individualized in series, does indeed have a different geometry in each assembly situation, however, the production process is identical for each part. A digitally continuous workflow from the 3D model to the data set for the CNC milling machine minimized the additional effort and cost which the differentiation of the profiles brought

with it. Each profile was given a clear identification in the form of a sticker which gave details of the assembly location and orientation. This information was of crucial importance to the assembly process and made additional plan documents for this working step superfluous. Differentiation within a series is only possible through the use of computers. Large quantities of data can be worked through exactly and automatically at much higher speeds than a human could manage. A new formal and technical quality arises, initially through the sheer quantity. As a result the focus for designers is shifted from generating digital or

physical objects to defining and controlling digital processes, which can then run in as many different iterations as desired.

Klaus Bollinger,
Manfred Grohmann, Oliver Tessmann

Notes:
[1] Wachsmann, Konrad: The turning point of building. Wiesbaden 1959 (English translation 1961), p. 83
[2] ibid.
[3] ibid., p. 84
[4] Haller, Fritz: System design Fritz Haller – Buildings – Furniture – Research. Basel 1989, p. 84
[5] ibid.

9

National Temple of Divine Providence in Warsaw

Architects: Szymborski & Szymborski
Structural design: Nazbud, Warsaw
Contractor: Warbud, Warsaw
Completion: anticipated for 2013

As a finishing element to the Royal Route in Warsaw, which begins at the castle in the Old Town, a new church is being built. Simple overlapping geometric hopes dominate the building layout: a circle as a symbol for God and heaven, a square as a symbol for the earth and a Greek cross as a symbol for Christ. Inclined pillars arranged in a circle, which converge in the dome of the building, mark out the nave. The whole construction of the building is conceived as a reinforced concrete support structure in exposed concrete quality, in order to give the space the necessary atmosphere of concentration on the essentials. With its internal inclined pillars from the framework construction and the altar wall, the "bell wall", the nave is particularly interesting and sophisticated from an engineering point of view. Due to its complex geometry the building could be neither planned nor constructed without digital methods. The design of the formwork and concrete reinforcement as well as the construction project management all took place in a completely computer-based way.

The architects' design was created with the help of hand-drawn sketches, physical models and digital modelling. Using the concept the architects explored the spectrum which ranges between rationality, design quality, ecology and further parameters from the target matrix. Modern building construction technologies, such as concrete reinforcement in a modular construction system in connection with CNC-controlled machines for the production of components, new flowing concretes, and high-performance concretes or bolted reinforcement splices, enable the realization of very slender construction parts in almost any design required. The technological

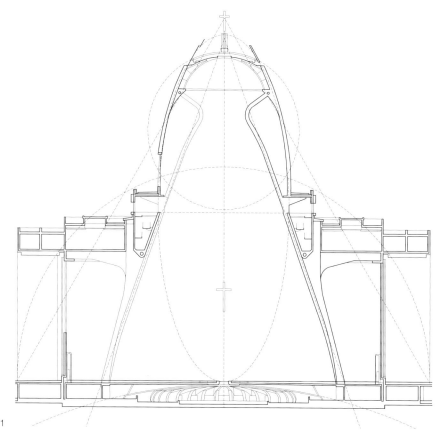

1   Section through the nave showing the inclined pillars
2, 3   Visualization of the cathedral
4   External view during construction

2

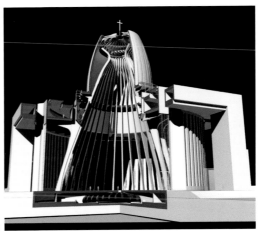

3

4

5

advance of formwork technology allows the economical realization of sophisticated geometries. The dimensioning and application planning in formwork technology are carried out almost exclusively digitally.

The complex geometry of the temple was construed by the architects in Auto CAD, both in a 2D and a 3D environment, and was made available to all involved in the project in the form of dxf/dwg geometry data as the basis for further processing. Construction information is transmitted to the construction site in the form of plans and geodesic checkpoints.

The nave of the temple is formed by a combined framework slab construction whose most distinctive feature is its 26 inclined internal pillars. They have a variable, structured cross-section and converge at a height of 59.20 m. An inner ring in the form of a rounded triangle and a bracket form the support for the dome construction. The formwork design is divided into two fundamental working steps. First of all, the formwork was designed using company-specific software provided by the formwork supplier. In the following step the individual components were dimensioned with the aid of another program (Robot Millenium). This program is linked with a manufacturer database which catalogues both elements of the modular construction system and other standard components from the fields of steel and timber construction. First, the supplier of the formwork processes the architect's dwg drawings, of the architect initially with their own software, and then transfers the data manually into the dimensioning software. Unfortunately, the flow of data is still affected by redundancies and manual interventions into the data structures. A standardization of the exchange formats will in future lead to

a considerable increase in efficiency. As the first stage of the construction, the internal inclined pillars were erected. Until they reached the support at a medium height and were able to be connected to the ring anchor above the external supports, they were structurally unstable. This is why a temporary steel space frame construction (fig. 5) with a diameter of 33 m and a height of 20 m in the interior of the building absorbed the forces in different construction situations. The space frame forms the substructure for the ground formwork which was layered with panel formwork.

Recess units on the panel formwork elements define the final form of the pillars. The recess units are produced in a workshop on the basis of computer drawings plotted in 1:1 scale. Alongside the complex formwork construction, guiding the reinforcement is another challenge. It must not inhibit the slenderness of the construction part and is thus partly executed using bolted socket joints which prevent the steel reinforcement overlapping.

A curved free form made from reinforced concrete forms the altar wall. With this the architects create the impression of flowing material. As was already the case in the design of the supporting pillars, this construction part was also developed with Auto CAD and the data, as the basis for production with suitable construction materials and systems, were transferred to the constructing engineers (fig. 6). These data form the basis for the computer modelling of the formwork body. Its components are precisely prefabricated with the aid of CNC-controlled mills and joined together to create formwork bodies. On the basis of the construction parameters such as construction time, resource arrangement of appliances or budget, the complete planning of the

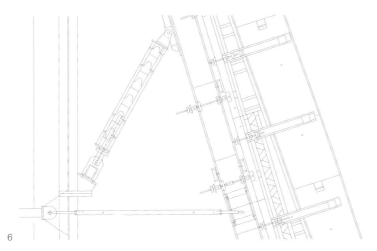

6

7

8

9

formwork implementation is developed digitally. However, despite precise prefabrication, a great deal of craftsmanship and skill is needed in order to be able to create an exact negative form of the freely formed concrete body.

The formwork concept implements the geometry of the free form in a realization of the construction part in several stages at different heights. Here, a so-called articulated wall-formwork is used which is particularly variable due to its smoothly gradated adaptability and was developed for the construction of curved reinforced concrete constructions. Recess units are positioned on the articulated wall-formwork, which generate the curvature of the construction part geometry. The components of the recess units – wooden cleats and formwork shell slabs – were generated using the software of the manufacturer in the same way as the oblique pillars. Due to the complex geometry, it was necessary to construct every single wooden cleat of the recess units individually and then to finish them with CNC-controlled wood processing machines (fig. 10, p. 90). Digital geodesic checks were carried out after the construction of the shell as well as during and after the concrete placement in order to make sure that the free forms are true to size.

The trend for more and more slender and hence significantly more heavily reinforced construction parts as well as the design of construction parts as free forms is leading to the development of new flowing, easy-to-work concretes which require no or only a small amount of energy to compact them. This property simplifies processes on the construction site and eliminates a potential source of quality impairment. This is why its use is recommended above all in exposed concrete constructions.

A particularly interesting construction material is self-compacting concrete (SCC), whose flow diameter is > 700 mm. This concrete does not require any energy to compact it as it is able to expel entrapped air using its own weight whilst being poured into the formwork. It is produced in concrete mixing assemblies which are computer-controlled and equipped with sensors in order to exactly determine the water content of the additives.
The material costs for flowing concretes are significantly higher than the material costs for conventional vibrated concretes. The price per m³ of concrete for a self-compacting concrete can be three times as much in comparison. However, rationalizations in the processing procedures, amongst other things as a result of the reduction of the number of workers within the working system as well as compacting machines no longer being required, compensate these higher costs.

In the early project phases (design phase), the architect and structural engineer should be involved in the project organization, which is determined by the contractual structure specified by the commissioning client, and criteria such as the following ought to be considered: [1]

5 The Temple under construction
6 Steel construction for supporting the formwork, and first stage of production
7 View of the formwork shell of the altar wall
8 Inclined pillars with formwork
9 Self-supporting inclined pillars without formwork

Digital processes

CAD construction part modelling

Production processes

Selection of system/construction material

CNC machine production

CAD modelling of the negative form (formwork)

Basic assembly of the formwork

Formwork implementation planning

Setting up the formwork

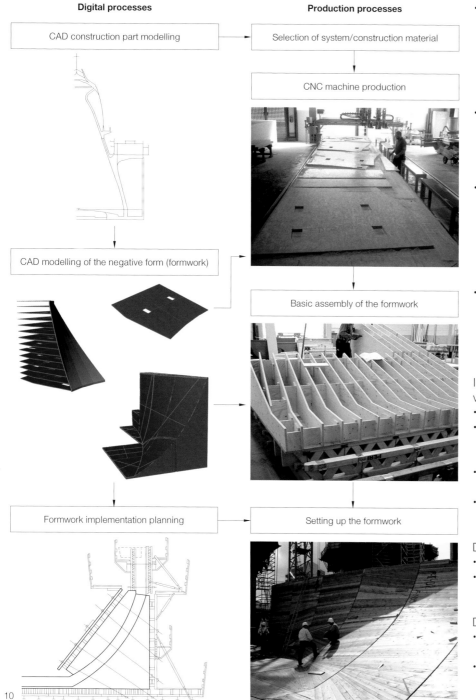

10

- Formwork construction technology: advice on the selection of formwork systems (including load-bearing capacity in agreement with the concrete technologists, formwork shell, formwork anchor and – if necessary – recommended concrete-separating agents)
- Concrete technology: advice on mixing design, integration requirements, integration capacity, arrangement of the construction joints, after-treatment, concrete-separating agents
- Concrete production and supply: quality of the materials going into the concrete, conditions for mixing, supply and consumption cycle of the fresh concrete, compatibility of the concrete with the concrete-separating agent and the formwork shell
- Construction: qualified advice relating to the basic conditions and demands of construction implementation (construction site) even if the contract has not yet been selected

In the formwork model plan the following variables should be given:
- Details on the chosen formwork system
- Arrangement and construction of the formwork elements (formwork element joints)
- Arrangement of the formwork shell joints
- Arrangement and construction of the anchors and anchor locations.

Details relating to the formwork shell:
- Type and quality of formwork shell
- Construction of the formwork shell fastening.

Details relating to the joints:
- Arrangement and design of the construction joints
- Arrangement and design of construction part/details relating to expansion joints

- Arrangement of further planar divisional elements (e.g. shadow gaps)
- Construction of edges, blind anchors, built-in parts.

Tolerances
- Permissible dimensional tolerances according to standards (DIN 18 202).

Further details
- Permissible pressure of green concrete.

Through the combined progress in graphic data processing, in concrete and reinforcement technology as well as formwork technology, today there are no limits in designing reinforced concrete construction parts. The level of precision is high-owing to modern measurement technology as the construction parts are subjected to permanent monitoring throughout construction. As the ongoing development of concrete and formwork technology constantly simplifies execution, complex construction parts adapted to specific structural situations are being used more and more.

Christoph Motzko

Note:
[1] GSV publication: Recommendations for Planning, Tendering and the Use of Formwork Systems in the Execution of "Concrete Surfaces with Special Requirements for Appearance", Ratingen/Darmstadt 2005

10 Computer-based workflow of a formwork construction process
11 Form after completion, with exposed concrete   11

Taichung Metropolitan Opera House in Taiwan

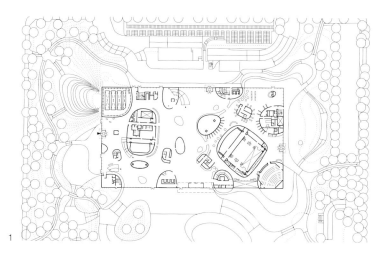

1

Architects: Toyo Ito & Associates, Architects
                (TIAA), Tokyo
Completion: anticipated for 2014

The design concept for the Taichung Metropolitan Opera House stems from a competition design from the architects of the Ghent Cultural Forum (GCF) from 2004 (fig. 4 and 5). The concept does not conceive the idea of a cultural centre as a separate place but rather as part of the city. The combination of the so-called City Cavity and Sound Cavity is developed starting with the location and not "imposed upon the place". The straight-lined urban city structure in Taichung is contrasted by a public park and enables an open city space out of which the actual City Cavity develops (fig. 1). The

watercolour by Toyo Ito shows his vision of a building structure which is criss-crossed horizontally and vertically by enclosed paths (fig. 6). The City and Sound Cavities, along with the connections to the park and roof garden, create flowing transitions between the interior and exterior.

Toyo Ito formulates his design vision with a clear statement on the potential of digital technologies: "The architecture I strive for changes Euclidean geometry to a non-linear geometry which is based on nature, because I feel that humans are

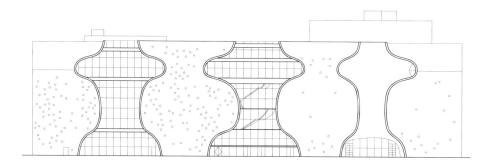

2

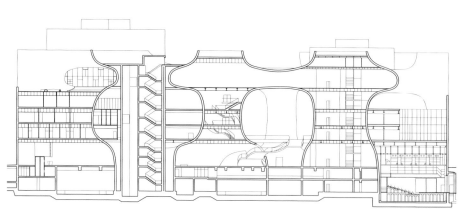

3

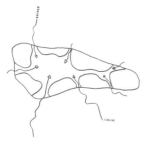

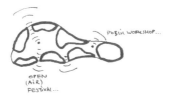

4

5

losing their sensitivity and vitality in the ubiquitous grid-formed urban and architectonic spaces. Computer technology liberates architecture from Euclidean geometry. It enables the realization of the instable flow of moving bodies and the complex balance of growing plants in the architectonic space. In today's world buildings are reduced to "commodities" in the structures of the economy and the information media; what we are looking for in architecture are spaces which are genuinely vital, which physically capture us. Now, as I am preaching a return to the past, I am using the new technologies to

realize the 'new genuine' dream beyond modernism." [1]
The design process for the Taichung Metropolitan Opera House demonstrates all stages of digital design from the digital translation of analogue sketches, software-based simulation and optimization to computer-controlled production of the construction. The complex building concept could not have been implemented without digital methods. Formfinding by means of minimal surface programs, optimization of the supporting structure using simulation software, and the use of acoustic parameters for

1 Newly laid out park which embeds the opera house in context; the transitions from building to green space are fluid and orientate themselves on Mies van der Rohe's visions of open space where the boundaries between the interior and exterior are removed. Scale 1:2500
2, 3 Sections
4 The urban grid is adapted to the internal and external conditions and forms the City Cavity.
5 Competition model of the project's forerunner for the city of Ghent, which strove to achieve a smooth linkage with the old town
6 Analogue working method of Toyo Ito in the form of hand-drawn sketches which appear virtually three-dimensional
7 Digital transformation into spatial computer models

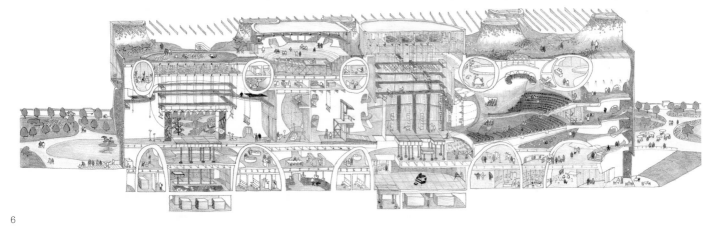

6

7

8

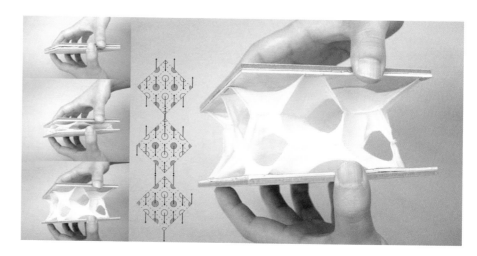

determining geometry are indications of a fully integrated computer-based design process.

The completely new spatial design creates flowing transitions between the floor, wall and ceiling; the spaces flow into one another (fig. 13). The inspiration for the development of this form lies in concept models (fig. 8) in which spread membrane surfaces generate a continuous spatial structure. In order to use the room program as a guideline for design, a structural system is required which reacts flexibly to alterations across the whole

design process. The result is a structure which adapts to internal and external constraints like a living organism. The organizing pattern is no longer Cartesian but self-generating (emergent) and organic.

A single specialist carries out the 3D modulation. After all designers and engineers involved have carried out investigations in their area, the minimum functional requirements are combined in a computer model and the program surfaces are checked for overlap. In order to translate the sophisticated geometry into a man-

ageable design process, initially, a rough grid of circles is developed which separates City Cavity and Sound Cavity from one another in an alternating way length- and cross-wire (fig. 14). For optimal spatial and structural dimensioning, a spatially abstract digital model called a Voronoi raster model is created (fig. 15). The effects of locally required adaptations to the floor plan on the overall structure are controlled by the active points of the digital building model. The active points are associatively networked with the model structure which surrounds them, which means that alterations have

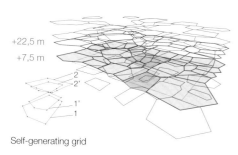

+22,5 m
+7,5 m

Self-generating grid

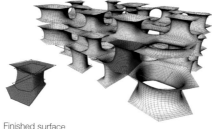

Finished surface

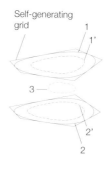

Self-generating grid

Loft

10

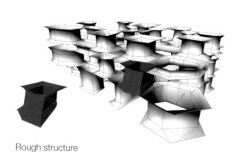

Rough structure

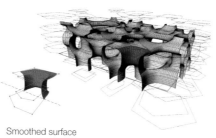

Smoothed surface

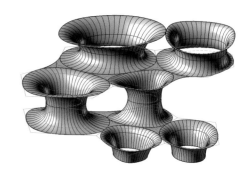

9

11

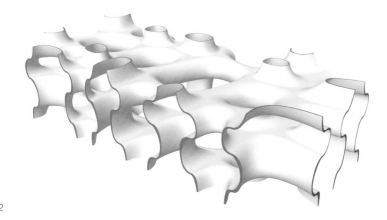

12

an effect on all the points. The interim steps are regularly superimposed with the room program (fig. 16), then transferred into individual three-dimensional construction parts (fig. 17) and smoothed. This method is efficient in terms of calculating and results in similar, continually repeating minimal surfaces, the so-called catenoids. They form both individual spatial zones as well as effective support structure parts. By stacking them, the overall body of the opera house is created (fig. 9). Finally a smoothing algorithm generates the flowing appearance of the interior space (fig. 10).

As the opera house is a public space, a complex structure arises which has to fulfil structural considerations, safety aspects, acoustic requirements, and criteria relating to comfort. The development of the building and its structural design are directly dependent on one another. An overarching data model visualizes resulting requirements and consequences. The basic construction is made up of the catenoids described which are geometrically controlled via the Voronoi model. In order to optimize the overall structure the wall thickness of the catenoids is minimized. The geometry has

8 Basic principle of spatial formation in the model
9 By stacking and adding the catenoids, an overall structure is created from individual parts which are then smoothed into a structure in a separate calculation process. With each alteration to an individual part there is a parametrically coupled alteration to the overall system. As this process is frequently repeated and very intensive in terms of calculations, an abstract Voronoi raster with control points is used.
10 Smoothing procedure of an individual catenoid
11 The addition of several catenoids
12 3D model of the surface
13 Rendering of the interior space
14 Evenly spaced grid with circles
15 Flexible grid: self-generating grid
16 Initial grid on a rough plan
17 Stacking tier of the self-generating grid

14

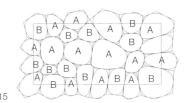

15

16

13

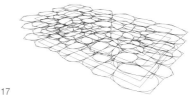

17

maximum construction efficiency if perpendicular elements are avoided, as the multi-directionally curved construction parts form a surface-active supporting structure without high notch stresses. Therefore, a traditional arrangement of wiring in ceilings and shafts is not possible which is why the wiring arrangements need to be developed separately and spatially checked.

Each alteration to individual components has consequences for the whole structure. A parametric overview model controls these complex interdependencies.

At an early stage of the project the architects link the structural development of the overall model with a finite element calculation from the structural engineer, Arup, and optimize it constructively as needed through geometric alteration. As, to date, there is no prototype for a reinforced concrete construction of this type, Arup developed a new optimization algorithm which reduced the quantity of concrete of the catenoid walls and the quantity of steel reinforcement. The comprehensive calculations require the use of high-power computers. The isometry in fig. 18 shows the support structure

stresses which arise if individual catenoids are simply overlaid and always constructed with the same wall thickness. In order to compensate for these tensions, the wall thickness and concrete reinforcement need to be adapted to each situation. Initially, relatively thick catenoid walls are assumed in the dimensioning due to the tight curvature radii. The finite element model analysis shows that the dead weight of the massive walls has a negative effect. Subsequently, the wall thickness for each individual case is calculated and dimensioned. The dead weight can be reduced by inserting light-weight

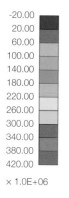

-20.00
20.00
60.00
100.00
140.00
180.00
220.00
260.00
300.00
340.00
380.00
420.00

$\times$ 1.0E+06

18

19

20

21

solid bodies whilst retaining the same construction height.

The geometry of the catenoids and, ultimately, of the construction itself is adjusted to the requirements of the secondary system. For this, lifts, vertical shafts and escape routes are arranged between the catenoids (fig. 19–21). Information from these secondary construction components such as, for example, tension regulations for earthquake safety, is also incorporated in the structural model; finally, on the basis of all the pieces of information, the structural analysis is carried out. Following the form-

finding of the catenoids, further structural parameters such as, for example, concrete reinforcement cross-sections, are established.

Despite the seemingly perfect simulation options on the computer, an analogue model is still the quickest way of checking space and architecture and achieving consensus on the design objectives. For this reason the architects created physical models in parallel with the virtual simulation. Free forms can only be inaccurately manufactured in an analogue process, whereas digitally controlled model construction technologies are

18 FEM analysis
19 Structural model with smoothed walls
20 Tension diagram of the catenoid structure
21 Structural model with vertical shafts
22 Competition model created in a rapid prototyping procedure, at a scale of 1:200
23 The interior spatial model at a scale of 1:100 was also created from aluminium wire mesh.
24 Commercially available styrodur sheets (t = 10 mm) are cut to size with a cutting plotter, glued, and processed manually into homogenous surfaces – scale 1:100.
25 Model (scale 1:50) made from commercially available 20-mm-thick styrodur sheets cut out with a cutting plotter.

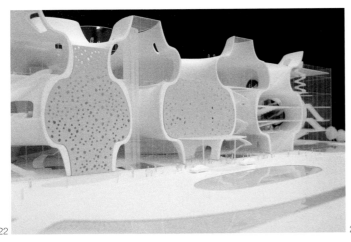
22

23

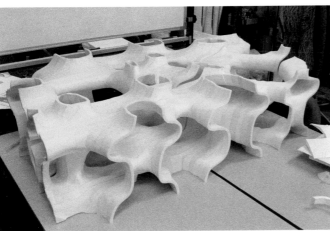
24

25

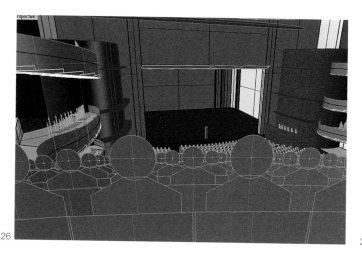

26

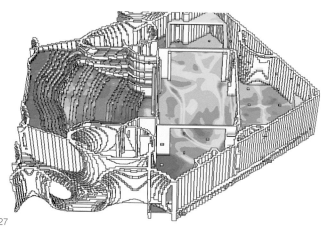

27

quicker, more flexible and more precise. In the competition phase TIAA used rapid prototyping procedures whereby CAD design provided the data for controlling the plaster plotter. As rapid procedures (see chapter "Production technologies") are limited in terms of size, CNC mills, CNC cutting plotters and CNC laser cutters, which allow larger construction parts to be produced, were also used in the further development of the project. These parts are then crafted by hand and joined together. Thanks to these parallel analogue and digital methods the Toyo Ito team received quick feedback in the course of the design.

The building services planning of the large opera hall is particularly complex due to the variety of requirements. The

different teams of engineers each use specific programs. Alongside carrying out an air conditioning simulation, lighting scenarios, light and evacuation paths are calculated and optimized using simulation software. The aspects of the individual simulations are combined in a large data model.

In an opera house perfect acoustic spaces are required. Initially, the form of the large opera hall is developed based on functional criteria for visitors such as infrastructure provision and viewing axes. The statically expedient curvature radii for the room shell resulting from this are then aligned with the requirements in terms of building acoustics, the aim of which is to optimize the sound direction and reverberation times. In order to achieve

a high acoustic quality, the sound must spread as a direct reflection. In order to realize this, the company Nagata Acoustics uses a computer simulation it has developed itself; with its help, seats with deficient or excessive tonal reflection can be identified. Based on the results, the overall form is partially modified and augmented by reflection walls. The acoustic simulation (fig. 28–30) visualizes the spread of the reflection using vectors, so that the layman can trace the path of the sound. In order to verify and improve the findings from the virtual simulation, an acoustic measurement walk-in model to a scale of 1:10 is made. The measurements in the model generally confirm the calculations of the acousticians. In order to improve the tonal quality, fine adjustments are made to the sur-

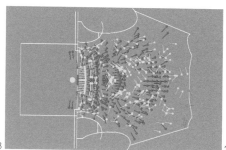

28

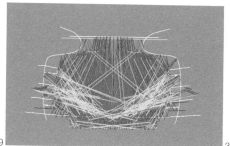

29

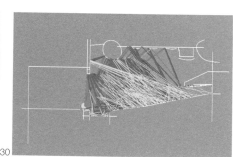

30

31

32

face geometry and material. The feedback loop between the computer simulation and the physical measurement model is an important part of the digital process.

In order to build the opera house, an efficient means of construction is sought for the elaborate geometry of the self-supporting catenoids. As there is no experience in Asia with comparable load-bearing concrete formworks of this size, from the start of planning an intensive exchange of ideas took place between Cecil Balmond from the Arup office and Toyo Ito in which different construction variants were analyzed. The simulations of interdependencies, which are difficult to capture, are not possible without computer calculations. At the beginning of planning, a formwork construction, made

from a load-bearing steel construction which has been cut with a CNC laser, was developed, which is enveloped on both sides by sprayed concrete. This construction defines the geometry. Complicated formwork is not used. However, a pure steel support structure proved to be too expensive. In the further development the use of a steel/concrete composite construction is planned. The sandwich construction consists of individually calculated rib-shaped beams, which dictate the geometry and wall thickness. They are cut from sheet steel using a CNC laser and then fitted with welded flanges. The formwork is assembled from a 2-axial curved concrete reinforcement (fig. 36, p. 100) and an expanded metal facework. The concrete reinforcement is closed with sprayed concrete. In-situ-cast concrete

26 Viewing axis simulation
27 Air flow simulation as a horizontal projection and in cross-section
28–30 Sound reflection analysis as a horizontal projection, cross-section and longitudinal section
31 Light simulation in a model 1:100
32 CNC mill creates the acoustic measurement model
33 Model 1:10 with CNC-milled substructure and manual planking in accordance with the exact stipulations for the measurement of sound and light paths and for the fine adjustments of the planar geometries and surfaces
34 Measurement model 1:30 primed and supplemented by manually produced furnishings and fixtures
35 Walk-in measurement model

33

34

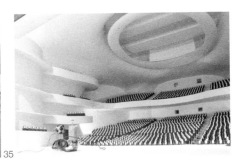

35

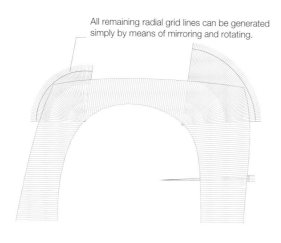

All remaining radial grid lines can be generated
simply by means of mirroring and rotating.

36

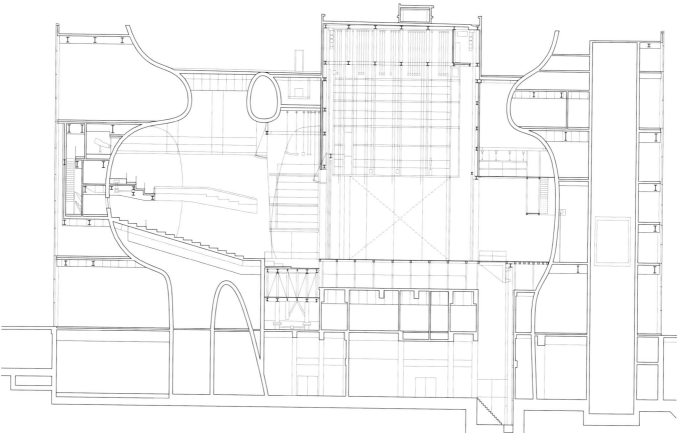

37

38

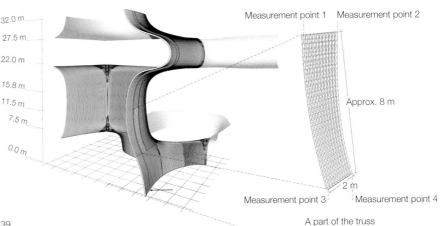

32.0 m
27.5 m
22.0 m
15.8 m
11.5 m
7.5 m
0.0 m

Measurement point 1 Measurement point 2

Approx. 8 m

2 m

Measurement point 3 Measurement point 4

A part of the truss

39

fills up the resulting cavity. Inserted hollow bodies partially reduce the mass. The shell form created is sealed with sprayed plaster and manually smoothed.

The section through the hall of the opera house shows that the technical fixtures are incorporated into the curved, load-bearing catenoid construction (fig. 37). The catenoids simultaneously serve the function of supporting structure, shell and wiring conduits. Each catenoid is optimized in accordance with its own requirements and differs in dimension and design. The permanent formwork made of sprayed concrete must withstand the

concrete pressure of the flowing concrete introduced. The assembly of steel beams with planking on both sides and concrete to form a spatially effective shell construction is called truss wall construction.

Before construction begins, a display model at a scale of 1:1 with a dimension of 2.2 m width and 3.5 m height serves to put the functionality of the new constructional engineering to the test. In the past, architects have realized constructions with multi-directional curved surfaces, albeit in significantly smaller dimensions. The complexity and challenge in terms of

36 Design of the form-defining concrete reinforcement
37 Section through the concert hall at a scale of 1:400
38 Prefabricated concrete reinforcement for the construction of a catenoid wall
39 Concrete reinforcement as form definition for the catenoid
40 Model of the interior space

40

101

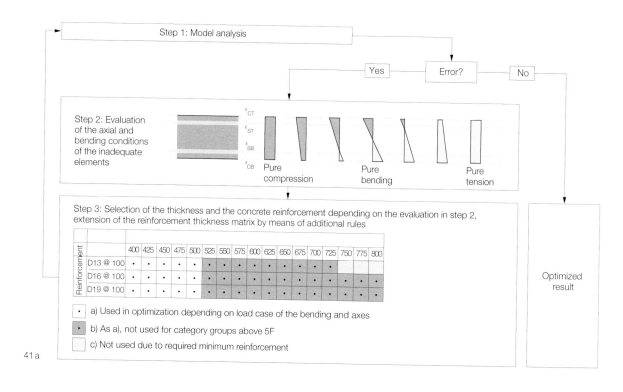

Step 1: Model analysis

Yes — Error? — No

Step 2: Evaluation of the axial and bending conditions of the inadequate elements

ε_{CT} ε_{ST} ε_{SB} ε_{CB}

Pure compression   Pure bending   Pure tension

Step 3: Selection of the thickness and the concrete reinforcement depending on the evaluation in step 2, extension of the reinforcement thickness matrix by means of additional rules

Reinforcement	400	425	450	475	500	525	550	575	600	625	650	675	700	725	750	775	800
D13 @ 100	·	·	·	·	·	·	·	·	·	·	·	·	·	·			
D16 @ 100	·	·	·	·	·	·	·	·	·	·	·	·	·	·	·	·	·
D19 @ 100	·	·	·	·	·	·	·	·	·	·	·	·	·	·	·	·	·

· a) Used in optimization depending on load case of the bending and axes

b) As a), not used for category groups above 5F

c) Not used due to required minimum reinforcement

41a

Optimized result

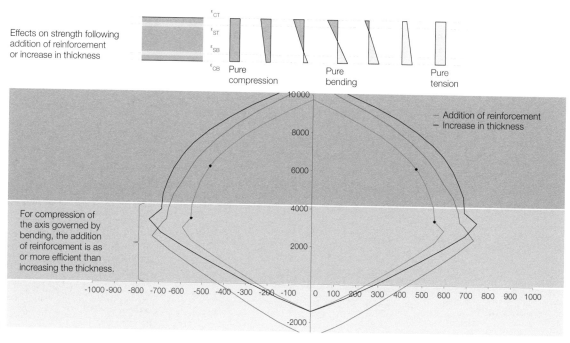

Effects on strength following addition of reinforcement or increase in thickness

ε_{CT} ε_{ST} ε_{SB} ε_{CB}

Pure compression   Pure bending   Pure tension

— Addition of reinforcement
— Increase in thickness

For compression of the axis governed by bending, the addition of reinforcement is as or more efficient than increasing the thickness.

10000
8000
6000
4000
2000
-2000

-1000 -900 -800 -700 -600 -500 -400 -300 -200 -100 0 100 200 300 400 500 600 700 800 900 1000

b

structural engineering of the opera house, however, surpass these by far. This is why a method is sought which enables the design planned on the computer to be implemented efficiently in construction. In the architectural design process we are continually faced with feedback loops to earlier design phases. Buildings with a simple grid system can be adapted to the altered conditions with little cost; however, in order to control the developmental path of a complex building, you need to design the transformation and modification processes very efficiently. The TIAA team developed a new design system, which allows simple adaptations to be made to the complex structure. The aim is not to generate one complex space, but rather an entirely new architectural system.

The organizational structure of the design process is very complex in this project. Its level of innovation and the execution in different countries – Japan (design), Taiwan (construction), and the UK (consulting) – require efficient and integrated software-based project management. This is why a fully integrated BIM (see chapter "Planning technologies", p. 35ff.) was installed which networked all the designers and engineers involved in real time and communicated alterations.
Shozo Motosugi and Yasuaki Mizunuma

Note:
[1] Translation based on: Futagawa, Yukio: Toyo Ito: Recent Project. Tokyo 2008

41 Optimization algorithm for the reduction of
    reinforcement
    a Optimization process
    b Analysis of solution
42 a Digital formwork planning
    b Preparation of the prefabricated reinforcement
    c Assembly of the fine-mesh reinforcement
       shell made from expanded metal
    d Application of the sprayed concrete
    e Finished mock-up in the support scaffold

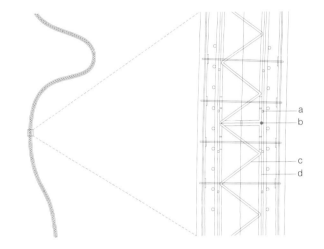

42 a

b

c

d

e

Glossary

3D laser scanning technology
Surfaces and bodies are measured using line- or grid-based laser scanning and are then translated into a digital volume model. The data can then be processed or used for generating an image.

4D simulation
With a 4D simulation the temporal construction sequence of the building construction can be visualized. Assembly sequences and interface problems can be better illustrated than with the classic schedule. The schedule is combined with the IFC 3D model based on object-oriented ways of working and thus enables 4D simulation.

Associative networking
The creation of a defined coupling of elements so that in the case of an alteration, all networked elements affected will be automatically altered too.

BIM (Building Information Modelling/Building Information Model)
describes the process of generating building data and managing it throughout the building's life cycle. Typically 3D/real time/dynamic building modelling software is used in order to increase productivity in building design and construction. This process produces the building information model (BIM for short) which encompasses the geometry, spatial relationships, geographic information and quantities and characteristics of building components.

Binary character string
is a unit of information composed of two digits (e.g. 0 and 1).

Blade
In tinsmithing a blade is a pre-profiled sheet (strip) with two upstanding lips on the sides.

Blob architecture
Constructions and designs which display complex, flowing and often rounded or biomorphic forms based on free-form curves (splines), and which only become conceivable for architects through the use of modern design software, are referred to as blob architecture, non-standard architecture or free-form architecture.

Brainstorming
is a method of finding ideas for generating new and innovative ideas in a group of people.

Catenoid
(also known as funicular or catenary curve) is a mathematical curve which describes the sag of a chain suspended from each of its ends under the influence of gravity. Catenoid surfaces are developed on the basis of a simple catenoid using rotation. The mathematical curve based on the rotation thus serves to develop a minimal surface with less surface and constructive volume consumption compared with right-angled systems.

Circularity
describes the central principle of cybernetic thinking.

Computational Fluid Dynamics (CFD)
is an established, approximate calculation method of fluid mechanics. The model equations used are mostly Navier-Stokes equations, Euler equations or potential equations. Computational fluid dynamics provides a cost-effective alternative to wind tunnel tests for complex cases.

Computer-aided (architectural) design (CAD/CAAD)
refers to computer-supported design or computer-supported construction. In this process the design is developed purely two-dimensionally (2D) or as a three-dimensional model of the object. In turn, conventional drawings can be derived from a 3D model.

Computerized Numerical Control (CNC)
Computerized numerical control is an electronically based method of controlling machine tools.

Conceptual map
As opposed to the classic mind map, relationships between concepts are more exactly specified in order to describe the type of relationship.

Cybernetics
The science of controlling and regulating organisms and machines, also defined as the art of control.

Data mining
stands for the systematic application of methods on a data inventory with the aim of recognizing patterns.

DGNB certificate
The DGNB certificate was developed by the German Sustainable Building Council (DGNB) in cooperation with the Federal Ministry of Transport, Building and Urban Development (BMVBS), which in 2001 published the sustainable building guidelines. It is awarded by trained DGNB auditors and evaluates the sustainability of a building through an examination of its economic, ecological and sociological aspects across its life cycle.

Efficiency
can be described as a ratio between the desired benefit and the cost invested to achieve it. The smaller the cost and/or the larger the benefit, then the more efficient the building process is.

Electro-pneumatic presses
combine electric component parts for controlling with pneumatic component parts (for example by means of electrically operated valves). The working medium (mostly compressed air) is controlled by electronic signals. Electro-pneumatic control systems allow significantly more complex functions, in particular through the use of electronic circuits such as, for example, programmable logic controllers.

Euclidean geometry
Euclidean geometry is the familiar geometry of planes, space and the objects contained within it (point, line, straight line, circle, polygon, sphere, etc.) along with their relations to one another (angles, parallelism, etc.).

Facilities management
is the term for the administration and running of buildings, plants and facilities.

Feedback
Feedback is a mechanism for amplifying or correcting a signal in information processing systems. A part of the output parameter is reintroduced in modified form to the input of the system.

Finite element method
With the finite element method phenomena of various physical disciplines are calculated. To do this, a 3D model is subdivided into any large number of parts, which are "finite" in number and not "infinitely" small. These elements are physically described by a finite number of parameters. The most well-known area of use is in structural analysis programs in engineering.

Flanging
is a forming and joining technique based on folding technology.

Flow map
Superimposition of a map with a flow diagram which illustrates the movement of objects from one place to another.

Form structuring
In contrast to form finding, a design technique in which the shell of the design is found using corresponding methods (see Frei Otto, for example), the form-structuring process defines the composition of the found shell in its components in accordance with design-based, structural and cost-relevant factors.

Fuzzy Cognitive Map
Mapping derived from fuzzy logic. FCMs are fuzzy, aligned graphs (digraphs) which, for example, represented as a matrix, make it possible to calculate the interdependencies of the factors of a project.

Generative design
The determination of the design takes place as a rule-based process, which is nevertheless open to any results, and thus leads to the further development of typologies in which questions of the form of the structure are solved, for example, by using shape grammars. Sub-disciplines: algorithmic, parametric and cybernetic design:
Algorithms (also solution procedure)
An exactly defined guideline for actions leading to the solution of a problem in a finite number of steps
Parameter (Greek: measure against, compare), also a form variable which occurs together with other variables but which has a different quality.
Cybernetics (from Greek kybernétes: helmsman) Explores fundamental concepts for the control and regulation of systems.

Genetic algorithm
Genetic algorithms deal with problems which are not analytically solvable by generating iteratively differing "proposed solutions". These can be combined with one another and a selection made until the stipulated requirements are more and more optimally fulfilled. As heuristically optimized procedures, genetic algorithms belong to the evolutionary algorithms. Areas of use are problems which cannot be solved in isolation or which are inefficient to calculate.

Geo/spatial information systems
serve to capture, process, organize, analyze and present spatially related information. They incorporate the hardware, software, data and applications needed for this.

Geodesy
(from Greek gé: earth, daídzo: I share) according to the classic definition from Friedrich Robert Helmert is the "science of measuring and mapping the earth's surface".

High-speed Internet
is a physical communication structure without an explicit Internet protocol. Also operated in Germany as XWin by the German Research Network, since 2006 the scaling potential has reached possible speeds of over 1000 GBit/s (1 Terabit/s).

Industry Foundation Classes (IFC)
are an open (software-independent) standard for the digital description of building models.

Iteration (iterative procedures)
(from Latin iterare: to repeat) is used for step-by-step, software-supported optimization of construction elements.

Jet cutting
In this procedure all the possibilities of form definition can be fully exploited. The CNC-controlled procedure is very precise and efficient. Depending on the material, parts up to 250 mm thick and a surface area depending on the size of the machine can be produced.

Leadership in Energy and Environmental Design (LEED)
is a classification system for ecological construction introduced by the U.S. Green Building Council in 1998. A series of standards were defined for environmentally friendly, resource-conserving, sustainable building.

Mapping

The term mapping describes the preparation and visualization of information on a numerical, written and graphical level.

Mind map

Describes a cognitive technique which can be used for visually representing a subject area, for planning or for taking notes. Associations are meant to help thoughts and ideas to unfold freely.

Mock-up

Etymologically speaking the term mock-up means a fake or dummy. As a scale model or replica the mock-up is used for presentation purposes. Famous from the aviation industry mock-ups are also used in industrial design and architecture for illustration and simulation.

Monitoring

Monitoring stands for the systematic capture and surveillance of a process using technical devices or other observation procedures. Repeat execution is key to each of the examinations in order to be able to draw conclusions from comparisons of the situations. The function of monitoring is as a guiding intervention into a process should an undesirable course of events be ascertained.

Mould

is the term used in compression moulding, forging or similar procedures for the form within which the material lies.

NanoLOC

Wireless sensor networks with decentralized data storage provide the basis for the determination of the positions of load carriers. Via the extended Kalman filter the unknown position of a load carrier can be found accurate to half a metre.

Nibbling

Production procedure (subcategory of punching) for perforating and processing sheet metal panels. Characteristic for this procedure is that generally complex forms are blank cut with the multiple CNC-controlled application of a simply formed tool.

Notch stresses

Notch stresses occur as bundle of stress trajectories where there are notches and ledges resulting from forces being redirected.

Orthophoto

(from Greek orthós: correct, straight, upright). A distortion-free, true-to-scale depiction from aerial or satellite images.

Parametrics/parametric software

These programs provide the user with the possibility of creating associative connections between geometries generated. Thus, they achieve a higher level of intelligence in the design process than traditional CAAD software.

Photogrammetry

provides a group of measurement methods and evaluation procedures for remote sensing (photos and measurement images), in order to define the spatial situation or three-dimensional form of an object.

Pictogram

(from Latin pictum: painted, picture; Greek gráphein: to write)
A single symbol which gives information through abstract graphical representations.

Plug-in

is a standardized program add-on which is most commonly offered as an optional download.

Proximity gradient

Representation of the proximity to each other through reduced spatial object distances. Enables a qualitative representation of the relationships.

Radiolarians

(Radiolaria, from Latin radiolus: small beam) are a group of unicellular living creatures with an endoskeleton made of opal (silicon dioxide, SiO_2) which belong to the eukaryotes.

Real Estate Lifecycle Management (RELM)

is a term from the real estate industry. It comprises the management of the design process, construction, operation and marketing of a piece of real estate. The life cycle ends with the piece of real estate being pulled down, dismantled or found an alternative usage for.

Real time

The timelines in a simulator can be condensed or stretched depending on what the aim of the representation is. If the simulation time corresponds to the course of time in the real world then this is called a real-time simulation.

Redundancy

(Latin redundare: overflow, to be available in surplus) refers to a case of overlapping or superfluity which is detected in simulations.

Relation

(from Latin relation: carrying back)
Particular relationships between objects which together form the structure of a system.

Reverberation time

Under the term reverberation time we understand the time interval within which the sound pressure in a space drops to a thousandth of its initial value following a sudden silencing of the source of the sound, which corresponds to a level reduction of 60 dB.

RFID technology

Radio frequency identity: identification through the capture of transmitted beams.

Scripting

The development of small program extensions which display the analysis of a variety of possible solutions to the architect.

Semantic network

has the same meaning as knowledge network. Representation using generalized graphs consisting of interconnected nodes (concepts) and edges (relation).

Semantic web

As an extension of the World Wide Web it makes use of the significance of information for computers. The automatic interpretation and further processing of information on locations, persons and things, lead to new informational relationships being built up. New relationships, which could not be seen before, can be uncovered as a result (serendipity effect, see below).

Serendipity principle/serendipity effect

refers to a coincidental observation of something not originally sought after which proves to be a new and surprising discovery.

Shear cutting

or shearing is the separation of a construction material by two cutters which pass across each other (DIN 8588). In doing this the construction material is separated by shearing forces.

Software as a Service (SaaS)

is a software distribution model which provides, looks after and operates software as a service based on Internet technologies.

Thermo-cutting

In this procedure foam can be shaped into the desired form using a heated steel tool and heat-sealed to other foam parts by butt-welding with heat reflectors.

Topological evaluations

Topology refers to the spatial relationships of geo-objects with one another (neighbour relationships). In contrast to geometry, which relates to their absolute form and location in space, topological relationships between geo-objects are independent of scales such as distance. The most important topological relationships between two geo-objects A and B according to Egenhofer are:
- A is a disjoint union with B
- A lies within B
- B lies within A
- A overlaps B
- B overlaps A
- A meets B
- A is equal to B

Viscosity

is the measure of the resistance to flow of a fluid.

Voronoi raster model

Division of space into regions which are determined through a specified quantity of points in the space, in this case called centres.

White Paper

A collection of proposals for a means of proceeding in a particular field.

Workflow

We often hear the term "digital chain" in conjunction with computerized construction processes that enable a trouble-free flow between draft design, detailed design and fabrication or construction procedures.

Zero energy system

A system which does not use any energy.

Literature:
Reference books and articles

Digital planning methodology

Agkathidis, Asterios; Hudert, Markus; Schillig, Gabi: Form Defining Strategies. Tübingen 2007

Aranda, Benjamin; Lasch, Chris: Tooling. New York 2005

As, Imdat; Schodek, Daniel L.: Dynamic Digital Representations in Architecture. Visions in Motion. London 2008

Balmond, Cecil: Cecil Balmond. Architecture and Urbanism, 06-11. Tokyo 2006

Bohnacker, Hartmut et al.: Generative Gestaltung. Entwerfen, Programmieren, Visualisieren. Mainz 2009

Chaszar, Andre (ed.): Blurring the Lines. Computer-aided Design and Manufacturing in Contemporary Architecture. Chichester 2006

Garcia, Mark: Patterns of Architecture. Architectural Design. Chichester 2009

Garcia, Mark (ed.): Diagrams of Architecture. AD Reader. Chichester 2010

Hensel, Michael; Menges, Achim: Versatility and Vicissitude. Performance in Morpho-Ecological Design. Chichester 2008

Hensel, Michael: Emergence: Morphogenetic Design Strategies. Chichester 2004

Hensel, Michael (ed.): Techniques and Technologies in Morphogenetic Design. Chichester 2004

Hensel, Michael; Menges, Achim; Weinstock, Michael: Emergent Technologies and Design. Towards a Biological Paradigm for Architecture. Oxon/New York 2010

Iwamoto, Lisa: Digital Fabrications. Architectural and Material Techniques. New York 2009

Kolarevic, Branko: Performative Architecture: Beyond Instrumentality. New York/London 2005

Liu, Yu-Tung (ed.): New Tectonics. Towards a New Theory of Digital Architecture. Basel/Boston/Berlin 2009

Lynn, Greg: Animate Form. New York 1999

Pottmann, Helmut et al.: Architectural Geometry. Exton 2007

Reiser, Jesse; Umemoto, Nanako: Atlas of Novel Tectonics. New York 2006

Sakamoto, Tomoko; Ferré, Albert: From Control to Design. Parametric/Algorithmic Architecture. Barcelona 2008

Terzidis, Kostas: Algorithmic Architecture. Amsterdam 2006

Veltkamp, Martijn: Free Form Structural Design: Schemes, Systems & Prototypes of Structures for Irregular Shaped Buildings. Amsterdam 2007

Wallner, Johannes (ed.): Advances in Architectural Geometry 2010. Vienna 2010

Zarzycki, Andrzej: 2006-07 Form Z-Joint Study Journal. Columbus 2008

Production technologies

Bechthold, Martin; Schodek, Daniel et al.: Digital Design and Manufacturing. CAD/CAM Technologies in Architecture. Hoboken 2005

Buchfink, Gabriela: Faszination Blech. Würzburg 2005

Corser, Robert: Fabricating Architecture: Selected Readings in Digital Design and Manufacturing. New York 2010

Garber, Richard; Jabi, Wassim: Control and Collaboration. Digital Fabrication Strategies in Academia and Practice, in: International Journal of Architectural Computing 04, 2006

Gebhardt, Andreas: Generative Fertigungsverfahren. Rapid Prototyping, Rapid Tooling, Rapid Manufacturing. Munich 2007

Gibson, Ian; Rosen, David W.; Stucker, Brent: Additive Manufacturing Technologies: Rapid Prototyping to Direct Digital Manufacturing. Berlin 2010

Gramazio, Fabio; Kohler, Matthias; Hanak, Michael: Digital Materiality in Architecture. Baden 2008

Hopkinson, Neil; Hague, Richard; Dickens, Philip: Rapid Manufacturing. An Industrial Revolution for the Digital Age. Chichester 2006

Kalweit, Andreas et al.: Handbuch für Technisches Produktdesign. Berlin/Heidelberg 2006

Kolarevic, Branko: Manufacturing Material Effects. Rethinking Design and Making in Architecture. New York 2008

Kolarevic, Branko (ed.): Architecture in the Digital Age. Design and Manufacturing. New York 2003

Leach, Neil; Turnbull, David; Williams, Chris: Digital Tectonics. Chichester 2004

Lefteri, Chris: Making It: Manufacturing Techniques for Product Design. London 2007

Leibinger-Kammüller, Nicola (ed.): Werkzeug Laser. Ein Lichtstrahl erobert die industrielle Fertigung. Würzburg 2006

Moussavi, Farshid: The Function of Form. Barcelona 2009

Thompson, Rob: Manufacturing Processes for Design Professionals. London 2007

Optimization processes

Addis, William: Building: 3000 Years of Design, Engineering and Construction. London/New York 2007

Bechthold, Martin: Innovative Surface Structures. Technologies and Applications. London 2008

Bollinger, Klaus; Grohmann, Manfred; Cachola Schmal, Peter: Workflow: Struktur-Architektur. Basel/Berlin/Boston 2004

Greco, Claudia: Pier Luigi Nervi. Von den ersten Patenten bis zur Ausstellungshalle in Turin; 1917–1948. Lucerne 2008

Kloft, Harald: Anschaulich: Tragwerksentwurf experimentell 2002–2007. Kaiserslautern 2007

Mattheck, Claus: Design in der Natur: Der Baum als Lehrmeister. Freiburg im Breisgau 2006

Nachtigall, Werner: Biologisches Design. Systematischer Katalog für bionisches Gestalten. Berlin 2005

Noorani, Rafiq: Rapid Prototyping. Principles and Applications. Hoboken 2005

Piller, Frank Thomas: Mass Customization: Ein wettbewerbsstrategisches Konzept im Informationszeitalter. Wiesbaden 2006

Polony, Stefan; Walochnik, Wolfgang: Architektur und Tragwerk. Berlin 2003

Sachs, Angeli (ed.): Nature Design. Von Inspiration zur Innovation. Baden 2007

Teichmann, Klaus; Wilke, Joachim (ed.): Prozess und Form natürlicher Konstruktionen. Der Sonderforschungsbereich 230. Berlin 1996

Weinstock, Michael: The Architecture of Emergence. The Evolution of Form in Nature and Civilisation. Chichester 2010

Material/responsive architecture

Beesley, Philip et al.: Responsive Architectures. Subtle Technologies 2006. Cambridge 2006

Douglis, Evan: Autogenic Structures. New York 2008

Schumacher, Michael; Schaeffer, Oliver; Vogt, Michael-Marcus: MOVE. Architektur in Bewegung. Dynamische Komponenten und Bauteile. Basel 2010

Spuybroek, Lars: Research & Design: The Architecture of Variation. London 2009

Journals

Arch+ 158, 2001: Houses on Demand

Arch+ 172, 2004: Material

Arch+ 188, 2008: Form Follows Performance

Manufacturers, companies and academic institutions (selection)

The manufacturers named in the publication and included in the following list are a selection of possible providers. All details are explicitly not to be seen as a recommendation; they are to be taken as examples and do not claim to be exhaustive.

In conjunction with this publication an Internet platform has been created which illustrates and expands on the contents and topics of the book in dynamic form.
www.parametricproduction.de

Companies (Manufacturing)

Rapid Manufacturing

Arcam AB
www.arcam.com

FIT Fruth Innovative Technologien GmbH
www.pro-fit.de

Materialise NV
www.materialise.com

EOS GmbH – Electro Optical Systems
www.eos.info

Z-Corporation
www.zcorp.com

Large-scale 3D printing

Monolite UK Ltd
www.d-shape.com

Contour Crafting
www.contourcrafting.org

CNC milling

p&p gmbh vectogramme
www.vectogramm.de

Schreinerei Luther joinery
www.schreinerei-luther.de

Handwerkskammer Freiburg
(Freiburg Chamber of Crafts)
www.c-forumholz.de

CNC Speedform AG
www.cnc-speedform.de

CNC cutting

TRUMPF GmbH + Co. KG
www.trumpf.com

POHL-Gruppe
www.pohlnet.com

Wassmer-Gruppe
www.wassmer.de

3D capture

Qubic
www.qubic.com.au

NextEngine, Inc.
www.nextengine.com

FARO Swiss Holding GmbH
www.faro.com

Virtual project room

conject AG
www.conject.com

Companies (Software)

ANSYS, Inc.
Ansys finite element calculations software
www.ansys.com

Autodesk GmbH, Autodesk Revit
www.autodesk.de

SmartGeometry Group
www.smartgeometry.com

Dassault Systèmes S.A., Catia
www.3ds.com

COMSOL Multiphysics GmbH
www.comsol.de

McNeel Europe, Rhinoceros – Nurbs Modelling
www.rhino3d.com
www.rhinofablab.com

Academic Institutions

Architectural Association London,
Digital Fabrication
www.digitalfabrication.net

IAAC – Institute for advanced architecture of Catalonia
www.iaac.net
www.smartgeometry.org

Berlage Institut Rotterdam, Associative Design
www.berlage-institute.nl

Digital Crafting
www.digitalcrafting.dk

Royal Academy of Arts Copenhagen,
Center for Information Technology and Architecture
http://cita.karch.dk

TU Delft, Architectural Engineering
www.tudelft.nl

Harvard University, Graduate School of Design GSD
www.gsd.harvard.edu/academic/mdes/technology_design.htm

TU Kaiserslautern, Architecture faculty
www.uni-kl.de/FB-ARUBI/wwwarch/index.html

RMIT University Melbourne,
Spatial Information Architecture Laboratory
www.sial.rmit.edu.au

Stuttgart University
Institute for Computational Design ICD
www.icd.uni-stuttgart.de

Stuttgart University,
Institute for Lightweight Structures and
Conceptual Design ILEK
www.uni-stuttgart.de/ilek

Stuttgart Academy of Art and Design,
Digital Design
www.de.abk-stuttgart.de

FH Trier, Department Digital Design,
Digital Conceptual Design,
Prof. Dipl.-Ing. Holger Hoffmann
www.toolboxtrier.wordpress.com

TU Wien, Geometric Modeling and Industrial
Geometry, Prof. Dr. Helmut Pottmann
www.geometrie.tuwien.ac.at/geom/fg4

ETH Zurich, CAAD
www.caad.arch.ethz.ch

ETH Zurich, Department of Architecture and
Digital Fabrication
www.dfab.arch.ethz.ch

Picture credits

To everyone who has helped with putting this book together, through licensing their pictures, giving permission for reproduction and through providing information, the authors and publishers would like to say a sincere thank you. All of the drawings in this book have been created in house. Pictures without credits come from the archive of the architects or from the archive of DETAIL journal. Despite intensive efforts we were not able to determine some of the creators of the photos and images, however, their copyrights are protected. We would ask you to keep us informed accordingly.

Title left, page 44, 51 bottom left:
Gramazio & Kohler, ETH Zurich

Title right, page 49 bottom:
Freedom of Creation, Amsterdam

Page 6, 101 bottom:
Christian Schittich, Munich

Page 10:
Fu Tsu Construction Co., Ltd., Taiwan

Page 16 top, 17 bottom:
Hosoya Schaefer Architekten, Zurich

Page 16 bottom:
Yarden Livnat, Jim Agutter, Shaun Moon, Stefano Foresti, University of Utah

Page 17 top left:
Doantam Phan, Ling Xiao, Ron Yeh, Pat Hanrahan, Terry Winograd, Stanford University

Page 17 top right, 18 top right:
UNStudio, Amsterdam

Page 18 top left:
Daniel Belasco Rogers, Berlin

Page 18 bottom left:
Arno Schlüter / Frank Thesseling, ETH Zurich

Page 18 bottom right:
Sven Mossberger, Hochschule Luzern / Zurich

Page 19:
Urs-Peter Menti, Iwan Plüss; Centre for Integral Building Technology, Lucerne University of Applied Sciences – Technology & Architecture

Page 20 bottom:
Michael Bruse, University of Mainz, Institute for Geography

Page 21:
after Alois Schälin, AFC Consulting AG / Urs-Peter Menti, Lucerne University of Applied Sciences – Technology & Architecture

Page 24 top left:
Arik Janssen, Lorsch / www.arik37.com

Page 28:
Laser Design Inc.

Page 34:
Motzko, C.; Heck, D.; Roth, O.: Schnittstelle Planung-Ausführung beim Gewerk-Fassade aus baubetrieb-licher Sicht. In: Lange, J. (ed.): Conference script "LeichtBauen", Technical University Darmstadt, 2003

Page 35:
GAEB Gemeinsamer Ausschuss Elektronik im Bauwesen

Page 36:
After Elsebach, Jens: Bauwerksinformationsmodel-le mit vollsphärischen Fotografien, Dissertation, Institute for Building Operations, Technical University Darmstadt, 2008

Page 37 top, 39:
Pflug, Christoph: Ein Bildinformationssystem zur Unterstützung der Bauprozesssteuerung, Disser-tation, Institute for Building Operations, Technical University Darmstadt, 2008

Page 37 bottom, 38:
Hanff, Jochen: Modellorientierte Softwareunterstüt-zung bei der Arbeitsvorbereitung und Bauausführung. In: Kassel-Darmstädter Baubetriebsseminar Scha-lungstechnik, 2009

Page 40:
Motzko, Christoph: IT-Simulation und Realität – eine baubetriebliche Betrachtung. In: Stiftung Bauwesen, issue 13, Stuttgart, 2008

Page 48 top:
Ogle Models and Prototypes Ltd., Letchworth

Page 49 top left:
MGX by Materialise

Page 49 top right:
Thomas Duval

Page 50 bottom:
Vollert Anlagenbau GmbH + Co. KG, Weinsberg

Page 52, 53:
Monolite UK Ltd, London

Page 56 bottom centre, 57 bottom right:
TRUMPF GmbH + Co. KG, Ditzingen

Page 58 bottom left:
Fa. Lungmetall OHG, CNC sheet metal processing, Mayen

Page 59 top:
STEP-FOUR GmbH, Wals-Siezenheim

Page 59 bottom:
Hans Pattist

Page 60 top:
Heide Wessely, Munich

Page 60 top right:
KUKA Roboter GmbH, Augsburg

Page 61 bottom:
TAMSEN MARITIM GmbH, Rostock

Page 63:
Thalmann Maschinenbau AG, Frauenfeld

Page 64, top:
Ursula Böhmer, Berlin

Page 65 top:
StaBiKon GmbH, Duisburg / www.stabikon.com

Page 66:
Heike Mutter and Ulrich Genth, Tiger & Turtle – Magic Mountain, Angerpark Landmark

Page 67 bottom left:
Inox-Color/Detlef Schobert, Waldürn

Page 67 bottom right:
Monika Nikolic /arthur, Cologne

Page 69:
gee-ly

Page 74:
Deutsche Bank, Frankfurt am Main

Page 77, 104:
Frank Kaltenbach, Munich

Page 81 top left:
designtoproduktion, Zurich / Stuttgart

Page 85:
Roland Halbe, Stuttgart

Page 88, page 90 (pictures):
Peri GmbH, Weißenhorn

Full-page plates:

Page 70:
Precast concrete component façade in binary code design, office building in Essen (D) 2005, Bahl & Partner

Page 104:
WAVE 0.18, parametric wood structure, architectural museum of Munich Technical University in the "Pina-kothek der Moderne" 2010, Schubert & Kaufmann

Index

3D surface model	28
3DP	49
4D simulation	35f.
Abrasive procedure	58
Active points	94
Aerial photogrammetry	27
Algorithm	
- evolutionary	73
- genetic	74
Analysis software	73
Archaeology	27
Architectural model building	56f.
Argon gas	54
Assembly of individual elements, robot-aided	50f.
AVA connection	22
Baroque	9
Beading	62
Bend forming	62
Bending	
- free	62f.
- transverse-force-free	62
Bending and straightening	62
Bending edges	64ff.
BIM	9, 22, 30, 35ff.
Blow moulding	46
Blow-torch cutter	56
Brainstorming	17
Building components labelling	25, 26
Building design	27
Building management	30
CAAD	21ff.
CAD	21ff.
Cadastral maps	15
Calculation, iterative	25
Capture, digital	27ff.
Carbon laser	56
Casting	46
Catenoid	95ff.
Certification	30, 39
Chain model	18
Character string, binary	74
Chirp spread technology	40
Circular form bending, free	62
Circularity	73
City Cavity	92ff.
Client	29, 33ff., 41ff.
Close-up photogrammetry	27
CNC	
- bending edges	64ff.
- hot wire cutting	59
- jet cutting	58f.
- laser cutting	56f.
- milling	60f.
- model-building laser	56f.
- nibbling	66ff.
- precast concrete elements	50
- punching	66f.
- tube-bending technology	66
Cold forming	62f.
Communication	29
Concept modelling	46
Conceptual map	17
Concrete technology	90ff.
Construction project organization	33
Construction with precast concrete components	46, 50
Contour crafting	46f., 52f.
Control polygon	78
Control, numerical	45
Cybernetics	73
Data chain	26
Data exchange	29, 31, 34
Data interface	46
Data mining process	18
Data source	14
Deep-drawing	62
Default	42
Degrees of proximity	17
Deliverability	42
Density analysis	14

Design process, classic	24ff.
Design review	39
Designing, diagrammatic	18
DGNB	30, 39
Diagrams of shadows	14
Die bending	62ff.
Die forming	62
Distortion of data	33
Documenting work	38
D-shape procedure	46f., 52f.
DTM	27
Due date	42
dxf / dwg format	22
École des Beaux Arts	7
École Polytechnique	7
Email gateway	32
Embossment punching	66
Evolution	73
Evolutionary process	76
Exchange format	22
Expansion	46
External high-pressure forming	68
Extrusion	46, 53
FDM	49
Feedback link	11
Feedback loop	22, 73
Finite element calculation/method/ software/model	18, 19, 52, 69, 80, 82ff.
Fitness	73ff.
Flanging	62
Flow behaviour	18
Flow map	16
FM system	29
Folding	64
Form structuring process	25
Forming	62ff.
Formwork	
- model plan	90f.
- technology	88ff.
Free form	
- bending process	65
- geometry	28
Free forming	62
Free internal pressure forming	68
GAEB	34
Gas cutting	54
Genome	74
Geographic information system (GIS)	14ff.
Geometry data	14
Geo-referencing	39
Gothic	7
GPS	18f.
GRP coating	59
Heat expansion coefficient	20
High performance concrete	86ff.
High-speed Internet	18
Hot-wire cutting	54
Hydroform	68
Hydroforming	
- bending	62
- widening	62
IFC	22, 30, 34
Image information system	37ff.
Individual solution	73
Industrialization	7, 83
Interface, digital	33ff.
Internal high-pressure forming	68
Iteration	73, 76, 77, 85
Iterative process	77
Jet cutting	54, 58f.
Joint liability	41
Jointed-arm robots	51, 61
Labour costs	11
Land registry data	15
Laser cutting	56f.
Laser scanning device	27
Laser sintering	48f.

LEED	30
Level of liability	41
Life cycle	
- analysis	20f.
- phase	35
Linkage information	24
Logistical usage	25
Loss of data	33
Macro-scripting	81
Map	
- Conceptual map	16
- Flow map	16
- Fuzzy cognitive map	17
- Mind map	16, 18
- Network map	16
- Radial map	16
Mass customization	8, 46, 50
Mass production	83
Master builder	7ff.
Material parameter	20
Melting cutter	56
Mero joint	84
Metal laser melting	49
Milling	54, 60f.
Model-building laser	56f.
Modelling software, parametric	72
Multi-physics simulation programs	19
Mutation	73
NanoLOC	40
Neodymium laser	56
Network diagram	17
Network, semantic	17
New combination	73
Nibbling	54, 66
Non-linearity	17
Operator	22
Optimization	18ff., 24
Orthophoto	15
Parameter database	19
Parametrics	24ff., 72
Photogrammetry	27f.
Pictogram	16
Planning map	16
Planning procedure	26
Plasma cutting	54
Plug-in	21f.
Positioning system	38f.
Presentation of spatial information	14
Preservation of monuments	28, 61
Pressure forming	62, 68f.
Primary shaping	62
Process chain	33
Process gas	56
Process programming	61
Production technologies	10, 45ff.
- Forming procedure	62ff
- Generative processes	45ff.
- Joining procedure	45
- Primary shaping procedure	46
- Subtractive procedure	10, 45, 54ff.
Programming	
- code	26
- language	24
Project	
- controlling	29f.
- management	29ff.
- organization	89ff.
Project room	
- classic	29
- participants	29ff.
- virtual	29ff.
Punch cutting	66
Pure water cutting	58
Rapid	
- manufacturing	46
- procedures	46ff.
- prototyping	46
- tooling	46
Rate of data transfer	31
Real time	

- algorithms	19
- analysis	18
Re-crystallization	62
Redensification potential	15
Relational depiction	16
RELM	29f.
Remuneration law	43ff.
Renaissance	7
RFID	39f.
Robotic layering procedure	46
Robots	50f., 61
Rococo	9
Role as trustee	41
Roll	
- bending	62
- shaping	62
Roll bending	64f.
Rolling	62
Room book	17, 29ff.
Rotational punching	66
SaaS principle	31
Scatter diagram	28
Script/scripting	19, 22, 24f., 74, 81
Security standards	31
Self-teaching	61
Semantic web	18
Semi-finished product	62, 65, 68
Sensor	39f.
Separation procedure, thermal	56
Shearing	54
Simulation	18ff.
- Acoustic simulation	18
- Air flow simulation	19
- Energy efficiency simulation	19
- Fire behaviour simulation	18
- Heating requirements simulation	19
- Light simulation	19
- Model-based simulation	18f.
- Spatial usage simulation	19
- Static simulation	19
- Thermal simulation	19
- Traffic flow simulation	19
- Ventilation simulation	19
- Virtual simulation	18f.
Sintering	46
SLM	49
SLS	48
Solution space	72f.
Sound Cavity	92ff.
Spatial allocation plan	17
Spatial statistics	14
Space utilization analysis	14
Sphere theory	43
Stereo-lithography	46, 48
STL format	46, 52, 60
Sub-process	26
Structural support	25
- analysis	25, 72
- analysis software	25, 72
- generation	72f.
Support structure model	82
Surface area model	82
Sustainability	30
Swing folding	64
Symbol	16
Teaching	61
Technical data	14
Tension forming	62
Terrain models	15
Thermo-cutting	54
Time savings	26
TLS	27
Torch cutting	54
Triangulation	66
Two-component system	52
User handbook, digital	39
User-friendliness	31
Variant generation	24
Visual programming	24
Voronoi raster model	94ff.

Warm forming	62f.
Ways of working, model-oriented	36
Wire drawing	62
Workflow	26, 29
Working, integrative	26
Written form	42